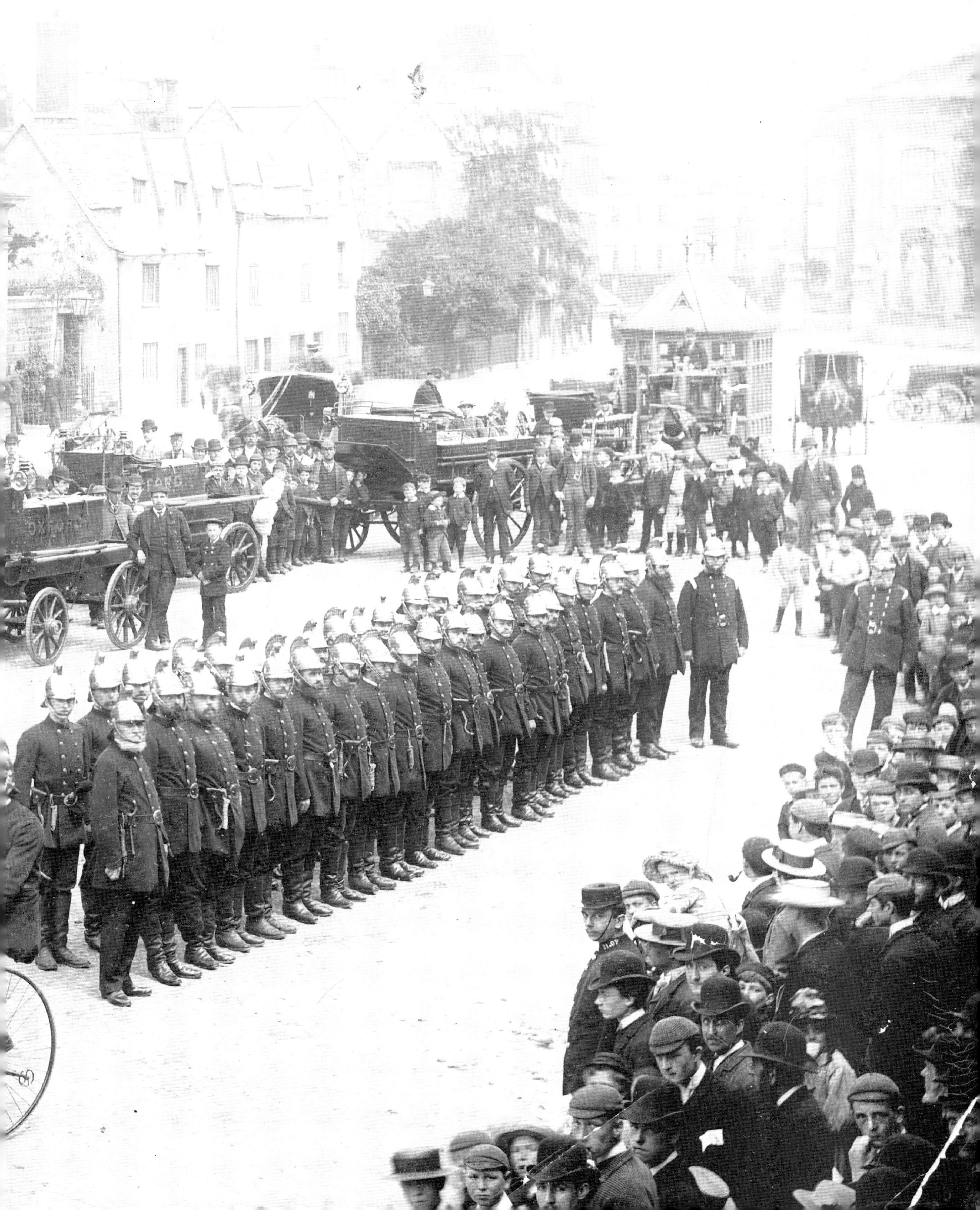
OXFORD

OXFORDSHIRE
of one hundred years ago

SIBFORD GOWER

ST GILES'S FAIR, OXFORD

OXFORDSHIRE
of one hundred years ago

ELEANOR CHANCE

ALAN SUTTON PUBLISHING LTD

First published in the United Kingdom in 1993 by Alan Sutton Publishing Limited,
an imprint of Sutton Publishing Limited

Copyright © Eleanor Chance 1993

Reprinted 1997

All rights reserved. No part of this publication may be reproduced, stored in a retrieval system, or transmitted, in any form, or by any means, electronic, mechanical, photocopying, recording or otherwise, without the prior permission of the publishers and copyright holder.

British Library Cataloguing in Publication Data. A catalogue record for this book is available from the British Library

ISBN 0-7509-0252-3

Library of Congress Cataloging in Publication Data applied for

ALAN SUTTON™ and SUTTON™ are the
trade marks of Sutton Publishing Limited

ST GILES'S FAIR, OXFORD

Typeset in 11/13 Bembo.
Typesetting and origination by
Alan Sutton Publishing Limited.
Printed in Great Britain by
WBC, Bridgend.

Preface

In this book *Oxfordshire of One Hundred Years Ago* my aim has been to bring together some of the best photographs and contemporary text to illustrate life in Oxfordshire at the turn of the nineteenth century. The area covered is that of the old county – before the boundary changes of 1974. Not every town and village is included but the spread is geographically wide and representative of the diversity of the Oxfordshire countryside, of its villages and market towns, of Oxford city and university, and of the lives of the people who lived there two or three generations ago. To give a fuller flavour of the period the photographs and text chosen date from the 1860s to 1920, but the majority are of the period from 1880 to the outbreak of the First World War in 1914.

In Oxfordshire we are very fortunate to have a collection of over 150,000 photographs kept by the County Council in the Oxfordshire Photographic Archive, and I must admit that it has been difficult to choose the 144 contained in this book from that treasure house. The Bodleian Library, too, has preserved a wealth of local material, including pamphlets, privately printed books, and ephemera that might otherwise have been lost. We are also lucky in the wide choice of excellent writers for this period. Flora Thompson and W. Warde Fowler write vividly of life in the villages; local newspapers give us insight into the day-to-day interests and concerns of local people (the motor car was already a cause of complaint in 1900). For Oxford there are abundant reminiscences and memoirs of city and university life: Sir Charles Oman tells us of the university police, the Oxford Alpine Club and the Revd Charles Dodgson (Lewis Carroll); Mrs Humphry Ward and Florence M. Gamlen describe social life, fashion, and the 'new race of married tutors'; and J.B. Atlay provides an account of Henry Acland, whose role as

SHIPLAKE

HENLEY REGATTA

physician and professor bridged the chasm between city and university created by centuries of antagonism. From the reports of the Oxfordshire Archaeological Society we learn of the traditional customs practised in rural areas: Pancake Day, Valentine's Day, May Day, Oak Apple Day, the dressing of the 'garland' at Charlton-on-Otmoor, and the morris dancing and bizarre mummers' plays. Perhaps the period was best summed up by the editor of Volume II of the *Victoria County History* in 1907 when he wrote: 'The flood of modern progress has overwhelmed the city of Oxford, but the rural villages have slept on, undisturbed in their peaceful seclusion.'

Drawing together the photographs and text for this book has given me a great deal of satisfaction and I hope that it will give much pleasure to its readers and stimulate their interest in Oxfordshire and its history. Finally I would like to thank the many people who have helped me with their advice, encouragement, and knowledge: especially Alan Crossley, Chris Day, and Christina Colvin of the Oxfordshire *Victoria County History*, Malcolm Graham and the staff of the Centre for Oxfordshire Studies, the infinitely patient Nuala La Vertue of the Oxfordshire Photographic Archive, and the Librarian and staff of the Bodleian Library.

Introduction

In 1902 H. Rider Haggard described Oxfordshire as 'exceedingly picturesque and even beautiful'. Before the boundary changes of 1974 the county covered just over 755 square miles, and within that area, a century ago, there were some 185,000 inhabitants. Over 60 per cent of them lived in villages, which were scattered fairly evenly over the whole area, rarely more than a mile or two apart. Old Oxfordshire had only one large urban centre, some 45,000 people living in Oxford itself; the next largest place was Banbury, with over 12,000 inhabitants in the town and suburbs. There were half-a-dozen other market towns with 3–4,000 inhabitants, then a handful of small towns such as Deddington, Bampton, and Watlington, which retained vestiges of their urban past – market squares, small town halls – but had become sleepy places, largely dependent on agriculture. Most had been by-passed by that crucial Victorian innovation, the railway.

For all kinds of physical and political reasons Oxfordshire was never a particularly closely integrated county. In shape it fell into two bulging parts, north and south, separated by a narrow 'waist', only 7 miles wide, where Oxford stands. The landscape is very varied, forming several sharply contrasting districts based on geological formations. In the far north are the rolling uplands of the 'red land' district, with their characteristic ironstone villages, and in the west the Cotswold country with its paler limestone; elements of the Cotswold landscape in attenuated form stretch eastward into the stonebrash of the Woodstock area and across the River Cherwell, even as far as Bicester. A dominant feature in much of the Oxfordshire countryside is the River Thames, which formed the old county boundary for some 74 miles on the west, running through flat, lush meadowland with willows flanking the main river and its numerous tributaries. East of Oxford the clay vale stretches to the distinctive former inland marsh of Otmoor. In the south of the county dense beech woods cover the chalk of the Chiltern Hills, and here, in contrast to the stone villages of much of

LEW CHURCH

OXFORDSHIRE *of one hundred years ago*

ROLLRIGHT STONES

Oxfordshire, are many timber-framed buildings finished with flint and brick.

The shape and varied landscape of Oxfordshire probably contributed to a division of its county community between several focal points. In the north, for example, Banbury was very much regarded as the centre of its own region, 'Banburyshire', which included parts of neighbouring counties; likewise in the south, Henley, separated from the rest of Oxfordshire by the Chilterns, had its commercial links with London rather than the Midlands, and probably regarded Oxford as, for most purposes, distant and irrelevant. It is debatable, too, whether Oxford, because of the dominance within it of the university, ever really had the same unifying influence as most county towns. Although it was a meeting place for the squirearchy during quarter sessions, races, elections and so on, it seems that they never took over the town's social life on those occasions as did their counterparts in, say, Shrewsbury or Dorchester. The country gentry never made Oxford a place of more than fleeting social gatherings, and probably they did not really feel at home in an atmosphere so dominated by university men.

The presence of the university, since its beginnings in the Middle Ages, affected all aspects of life not only in Oxford but in much of the surrounding countryside. A series of almost continuous disputes over the centuries had resulted in the university gaining a large measure of control over aspects of town life such as markets and fairs, rents, local government, policing, civil and criminal jurisdiction, and even public entertainments. Until the end of the nineteenth century Oxford was considered 'just so much of a town as was sufficient to minister to university wants'. Colleges owned much of the land around Oxford and in the county as a whole, enabling them to influence the growth, particularly close to Oxford, of new building development.

Oxfordshire historically was noted for being 'the best water'd county in England', with fertile arable, pasture 'as fine as any in England', and plentiful water-power on which its medieval woollen industry had been based. Much ancient woodland had been removed by the later nineteenth century, but a few impressive stretches survived, notably in the Wychwood area and the Chilterns. Another valuable resource of the county was stone; in 1907 there were still some forty quarries in use, many of great antiquity. By then, however, Stonesfield slate, created by the splitting action of frost on fissile rock, was becoming less popular: its cost made it difficult to compete with Welsh slates and clay tiles, and the last pit was closed *c.* 1911. Clay was worked for bricks and tiles in many parts of Oxfordshire, and iron mining in the north of the county continued into the twentieth century.

Oxfordshire's heavy dependence on agriculture resulted in declining population in the late nineteenth century, as the effects of the agricultural depression began to be felt. It was one of only four English counties to show no population increase in the 1890s, and in 1901 had fewer inhabitants than a century earlier. In most parishes land ownership had drifted into fewer and fewer hands; a series of poor harvests,

Introduction

MAY DAY, GREAT ROLLRIGHT

importation of food, and increasing mechanization all contributed to a reduced demand for agricultural labour. In some villages the population fell by 40 per cent and half the cottages were unoccupied. The younger generation left their rural homes for work on the railways or in the manufacturing towns; others, lured by promises of a brighter future, left for Canada, Australia, New Zealand, and South America. Some emigrants were assisted by the Agricultural Labourers' Union, others by their parishes. Even in 1909 local newspapers carried advertisements extolling the good life in the 'new world'. As J.M. Falkner remarked of Oxfordshire in 1899: 'the tale of struggling agriculture and dwindling population can be read easily enough in empty cottages . . . and toothless gaps in the village street where cottages have been altogether cleared away, and in the curious absence of children'.

Farm labourers were poor: at best their wages were between 12*s* and 14*s* a week. Working hours were from 7 a.m. to 5 p.m. with an hour for dinner; cowmen, shepherds, and horsemen often worked seven days a week. Annual hiring fairs, such as that at Burford, where labourers of both sexes sought employment with the highest bidder, continued into the twentieth century. In general the Oxfordshire labourer was regarded as worse off than his counterpart in the north of England. Some lived in tied cottages rent-free, but most paid weekly rents of up to 2*s* 6*d*. Large families were brought up in one- or two-bedroomed cottages; frequently the eldest child had left home before the youngest was born. Water supply and sewage arrangements were primitive, tainted wells and rivers commonplace. Child mortality rates were high, and in 1897 nearly one Oxfordshire baby in eight died before it was a year old. Most labouring families lived perilously close to subsistence level: the cottage or allotment vegetable garden, the chance harvest of the hedgerows, gleanings from the corn fields, the carefully nurtured family pig – all played a vital part in the rural economy.

There was considerable rural discontent, and Oxfordshire was prominent in the early years of agricultural trade unionism. In 1872 two Oxford academics (Professor J.E.T. Rogers and T.H. Green) shared a platform with Joseph Arch at a meeting to establish an Oxfordshire branch. Rogers, stressing that labourers must combine to improve their lot, reckoned that 'no combination had been so temperate or so hopeful as this one'. Even so bitterness and violence followed: unionists were evicted from jobs and cottages, and in 1873 there was rioting in Chipping Norton after sixteen women from Ascott-under-Wychwood were sentenced to hard labour in Oxford Gaol for intimidating youths drafted in as non-union labour. Although agricultural trade unionism in Oxfordshire collapsed in the 1890s it had achieved slightly higher wage rates and given the farm worker some self-respect. Astonishingly, labouring householders in the villages did not get the right to vote until 1884, and probably the agricultural union movement should be given some credit for that extension of the franchise.

PLUSH MILL, SHUTFORD

The spread of newspapers and improved communications had altered village life during the nineteenth century, but for most villagers the carrier's cart to their local market town provided the chief contact with a wider world. Some traditional feasts and local customs survived, and in most villages the parson, the squire (if there was one), and the larger farmers remained dominant figures. In the more 'open' kind of village, outside the control of a large landowner, there was a less subservient atmosphere, and here nonconformist chapels thrived. A great social influence in all villages was the school, which by late Victorian times was beginning to provide at least a rudimentary education on the basis of compulsory attendance. Literacy was improving, though schools were sometimes closed for weeks on end during outbreaks of measles, diphtheria or scarlatina; absenteeism, whether because of the employment of children on farms or in the home, or because of inadequate clothing in the winter, was being reduced by statutory enforcement. By the 1890s the funding of schools by grants based on results, which had led to a restricted syllabus and grinding repetition, had been abandoned. The 1902 Education Act gave the county and city authorities control of what had been the haphazard parochial provision of elementary education; at the same time secondary education was provided for out of the rates. Even so it was not until much later in the twentieth century that all Oxfordshire children were taught much beyond the three Rs, or that the poor gained regular access to secondary education.

In the market towns the traditional industries carried on much as they had in previous centuries. Brewing was particularly important in Banbury, Witney, Deddington, Henley and Oxford itself. Banbury's economy, flourishing for much of the nineteenth century, suffered severely from the agricultural depression in the surrounding area. Not only was it vulnerable as a marketing and banking centre for a predominantly agricultural region, but also its major industry, the Britannia Ironworks, which specialized in reaping and mowing machines, failed to diversify as sales diminished. The town's long-established plush-weaving industry had declined to workshop scale, except in the nearby village of Shutford. Here, however, it flourished for a time; power looms were

EIGHTS WEEK, OXFORD

introduced in 1885, and provided the scarlet plush supplied for the coronation of the last Czar of Russia. In Chipping Norton the tweed mills were one of the largest users of imported wools in the country. A disastrous fire in 1872 followed by the building, within twelve months, of a new mill, 'one of the handsomest in the land', provoked a financial crisis: in 1896 the Bliss family ended its 140-year long connection with tweed manufacture in the town. A divisive strike in 1913–14 attracted much attention in the county, as it was felt to be a test case for trade unionism in rural areas. When war was declared in 1914 many employees had been on strike for eight months, causing severe economic repercussions thoughout the town.

Probably the most successful industry in Oxfordshire was Witney's blanket manufacture, which, in contrast to most other undertakings in the county in the early twentieth century, was flourishing; in 1899 about eight hundred hands were employed and 250 looms were at work. In the area surrounding Woodstock, Chipping Norton and Witney the traditional cottage industry was glove-making. By the earlier twentieth century, however, the trade was diminishing; but at certain times of year the hedgerows were covered with sheep- and goatskins bleaching in the sun, and at cottage doors the women sat sewing gloves as out-workers for employers based in the towns. In 1904 over 2,000 women were employed in glove manufacture in this part of the county. Large-scale manufacture and purpose-built factories followed the establishment of railway links, which in Woodstock's case was not until the 1890s.

Henley's once profitable coaching and river trade had been lost to the railway, and its manufacture of malt had been usurped by towns nearer London. In 1896 it was described as 'not much given to manufactures, except beer and boats'. The River Thames, the basis of the town's earlier prosperity, was to be the cause of its revival. The first Oxford versus Cambridge boat race was held there in 1829, an annual regatta was established ten years later, and by 1851 had become Henley Royal Regatta. In 1887 a visit by the Prince of Wales gave it the ultimate seal of fashionable approval; some 34,000 people were said to have attended in 1895. An influx of middle-class settlers led to a revival of the town's service industries, and in the last three decades of the nineteenth century Henley's prosperity and population rose steadily.

In Oxford, besides brewing, employment was provided by the railway companies, two clothing factories, Cooper's

UNIVERSITY CRICKET

KEBLE COLLEGE

marmalade factory, Lucy's ironworks, building firms, and the University Press. Over a quarter of the working population was engaged in domestic service. By far the largest employer, however, was the university. For twenty-four weeks of the year (during term-time) it offered a wide range of casual employment to men and women – college servants, groundsmen, charwomen, and errand boys; but for the remainder of the year these people had to seek work elsewhere. In the vacations the colleges were almost empty, and except on market days (Wednesdays and Saturdays) the city was deserted; in summer the grass grew between the cobbles in High Street.

In fact the later nineteenth century saw dramatic changes in Oxford. From 1868 students were allowed to live in private lodgings. In 1870 Keble College was opened, its aim to enable men of limited means to gain a university education; its buildings, massive and described by the architect as 'gay' (red brick, banded with stone, and striped and chequered throughout with black and white brick), were in violent contrast to the traditional Cotswold stone of college buildings. In 1871 the abolition of religious restrictions opened the university to a still wider public. In 1879 the greatest revolution came with the opening of the first colleges for women, Lady Margaret Hall and Somerville, described by one senior academic as 'an educational development which runs counter to the wisdom and experience of all the centuries of

ENCAENIA PROCESSION, OXFORD

Christendom'. Two more women's colleges were opened before the turn of the century, although women were not actually awarded degrees until 1920. In the 1880s and 1890s two colleges were opened (Mansfield and Manchester) for non-residential students; and in 1899 Ruskin Hall (now College) was opened to make educational opportunities accessible to working men and women.

The university's rejuvenation increased the demand for shops, services and building work, cushioning the town from the agricultural depression that so severely affected Banbury. In 1893, for example, twenty-two new streets were under construction. A growing number of professional people were attracted to Oxford as an alternative to Cheltenham or Leamington – it was a pleasant centre for concerts, lectures, libraries and museums. Tourism began to play an important part in the city's economy. Oxford was especially celebrated not only for the beauty of its buildings but for its promenades and walks, both within and around the city. In this period the appearance of the city centre was changed by demolition, rebuilding and refronting; Queen Street, for example, was almost entirely rebuilt, and in the 1890s Oxford acquired a new town hall and corn exchange.

In 1881 it was remarked 'how very rapidly on all sides the town is extending its feelers farther and farther into the surrounding countryside'. The northern suburb, its spread boosted by a university statute of 1877 allowing dons to be married, was notable for its fashionable Gothic architecture. The architect William Wilkinson, sometimes described as the 'creator of North Oxford', came from a Witney family of builders and auctioneers. Besides the Gothic villas of North Oxford his designs can be seen in 'model' farms, churches, country houses, vicarages, schools and police stations all over Oxfordshire. By 1880 the eastern suburbs across Magdalen Bridge stretched along the Iffley and Cowley Roads as far as Leopold and Henley Streets. Across the River Thames, south and west of the city centre, in what was then Berkshire, housing extended towards Hinksey and Botley. In the 1880s Headington, Cowley, Iffley, Summertown and Wolvercote

ACCIDENT, ENSTONE

were still isolated villages, but by 1905 North Oxford had merged with Summertown. As the city's population grew a decreasing proportion, particularly in the poorer suburbs, was directly dependent upon the university for employment.

The later nineteenth century saw improved town–gown relations. In 1869 the university and city police were amalgamated; in 1876 T.H. Green became the first don to sit on the city council; in 1897 the university conferred an honorary degree on the mayor; and in 1913 a member of the university became mayor. The character of Oxford became less one-sided.

In 1899 the city's MP declared that 'the great need of Oxford is some large industry'. Only two years later William Morris (later Lord Nuffield) made his first bicycle at his father's house in James Street; ten years after that he built his first car, and by 1913 he was employing 300 men at the former Military Training College at Cowley. For some eighty years the car industry influenced the development of Oxford and Oxfordshire as deeply as ever the university had.

Old photographs invoke a powerful nostalgia for a way of life swept away by the changes of the twentieth century. With hindsight it is difficult to suppress a sense of impending doom – so many of those depicted were soon to endure a war that removed the flower of a generation and arguably destroyed for ever the confidence, optimism and respect for authority which had characterized Victorian life. The poet Philip Larkin, looking at photographs of young men going off to war in 1914, writes of 'the shut shops, the bleached established names on the sunblinds . . . the dark-clothed children at play, called after kings and queens', and concludes 'Never such innocence again'. Perhaps that awareness of looking back across a great divide makes us exaggerate the static, unchanging nature of life one hundred years ago. Certainly Oxfordshire observers of that period felt that in the county town, and even in the villages, they lived in stirring times, marked by flux and progress; the busy pages of the *Witney Gazette* reveal an ordered, but not an unchanging, world. Of course men's perceptions of the significance of innovations were sometimes amusingly naive. W.H. Hutton, writing of Burford at the turn of the century, claimed that 'Modern ways have not changed us much for better or worse. We have a parish council, but we are not very much excited by its doings. We have seen a motor car, and we don't think much of it. . . . We live very much like our fathers before us.' Even those who were aware that times had changed could hardly have foreseen that their world was soon to be altered almost beyond recognition. We can only smile ironically at W.W. Fowler's grudging concession that 'It is possible, even probable, that Kingham may see in the twentieth century changes as great as those of the nineteenth.'

OXFORDSHIRE
of one hundred years ago

FEBRUARY, 1909.

THE WHEATSHEAF

A MONTHLY CO-OPERATIVE RECORD & MAGAZINE.

ISSUED BY

STEEPLE ASTON
CO-OPERATIVE SOCIETY LIMITED.

C.W.S. Printing Works, Longsight, Manchester.

Several children were potato picking

SCHOOL INSPECTOR, NORTH ASTON

Teacher's Log Book

7 October 1893 – Ethel Davies went home ill yesterday, and I heard this morning that she has Measles.

The School Attendance Officer called yesterday – I told him that several children were potato picking; he said that it was useless reporting them, as the Magistrates would not fine the parents whilst Scarlatina was prevalent among the children.

The Sanitary Inspector called this morning, and told me that two children were suffering from Diphtheria, and when he reported the case he would probably close the school for several weeks. Besides some children being absent potato picking, others are gathering acorns for sale. Measles, Scarlatina and Diphtheria are among the scholars. – Teacher.

14 October 1893 – I enclose a formal certificate for the closing of your schools for 3 weeks. Please show the Certificate at once to your Committee. If any limewashing of the Schoolrooms or closets is required, I recommend that it be now carried out under any circumstances. I recommend that all woodwork in the schoolrooms and closets should be washed out with Carbolic acid soap, and that the closet vaults should be emptied and afterwards disinfected with lime. – Medical Officer of Health for Oxfordshire.

18 November 1893 – The Sanitary Inspector has called several times and brought Carbolic acid soap and other disinfectants to distribute among the people. He left some with me, and I have had the schoolroom floors scrubbed and washed with Carbolic soap, and I have made solutions of Carbolic acid and water to sprinkle over the floors occasionally. – Teacher.

20 November 1893 – School opened this morning after being closed for 5 weeks.

2 December 1893 – The children appear to have forgotten nearly everything they have been taught. – Teacher.

7 December 1893 – The undergraduates of Lincoln College are going to give a performance tonight in the School in aid of the School building fund.

Combe School Log Book

PUNTING ON THE CHERWELL

The Art of Punting

The punt is to the Thames what the gondola is to the canals of Venice. But a few years ago Mr Leslie regretted it was not more popular on the upper river. Now, wherever you go, you see the long straight boat with its passengers luxuriously outstretched on the cushions in the stern, the punter walking from the bow and pushing on his long pole. To enjoy his work he must know not only the eddies and currents of the stream, but something of the river bed as well. For this reason it is not easy to punt in unknown waters. Countless as were the punts we saw, I do not remember one laden as if for a trip. The heaviest freight was a dog, a baby, or a lunch-basket. As often as not a girl was poling, and I never ceased wondering how work, that looked so easy, could be as difficult to learn as punters declare it. But these are the three situations, I am told, which the beginner at the pole must brave and conquer before he can hope for ease and grace: first, that in which he abandons the pole and remains helpless in the punt; secondly, that in which, for reasons he will afterwards explain, he leaves the punt and clings to the inextricable pole; and thirdly, that of fearful suspense when he has not yet decided whether to cling to the pole or the punt.

J. & E. Robins Pennel.

St Giles's Fair

The land on which the fair is held is College property; and were it not that one knows that the annual rental brings in a large sum to the St John's coffers, it would seem strange enough that it should still be held in 'St Giles',' where some of the best houses and best families of the place are located, to whom the uproar and the turmoil of the fair must be a sad nuisance – added to which there is the imminent danger of fire from the numberless lamps, and lanterns, and cooking stoves, fed with highly inflammable oils, appertaining to the vans. We had some idea of what the horror of fire breaking out might be, from the rapid kindling and flaring up of a heap of small properties lying about a kettle hung over a lamp just filled from a huge paraffin can. The woman to whom it belonged flew like lightning to the spot, and whilst we were already picturing to ourselves the awful scene of a stream of flame running along the line of vans and canvas booths that stretched the length of St Giles', hemmed in on all sides, by crowds of sightseers and holiday-makers, many of them swinging high aloft in cars, boats, &c, she, equally alive to the danger, had caught the great vessel up in her sturdy arms and removed it to a distance. We had hastened to a point whence we might hope to get free of the surging crowd, if needful, as we passed on stopping some mothers with little children, and

ST GILES'S FAIR, DAY'S MENAGERIE

warning others not to approach. Our hearts beat fast as we watched the flames leap wildly into the air for the space of a minute or two. Then they succumbed to the efforts made to quench them, and probably few but ourselves and those in the immediate vicinity knew anything of the awful peril which that vast throng of persons had escaped. Had the preachers of the 'Church Army' band, who held forth to a small, changeful crowd during the whole time of the fair, seen what we did, they might indeed have found a vivid moral for their texts – 'In the midst of life we are in death.' 'My times are in Thy hands.' But the preacher did not see – he was too far off, and surrounded by a dense little crowd who were joining in singing a hymn. In the Bible and Prayer Book booth, near at hand, some country men and women were deeply immersed in selecting from the neat, darkly-bound volumes such as were to their taste; and a rough honest-faced fellow was handing over the small price of a copy as we passed. The 'sea-on-land' cars, with canvas sails full set, and a full complement of joyous, careless riders, were floating round and round with a motion so terribly true to nature that we watched the faces of the occupants, expecting them to turn grey or ashy white! But the steam whistle shrieked, and one set got out only to be replaced by another. Meanwhile, the braying organ belonging to a merry-go-round kept time with the prancing of wooden steeds and the dash of painted chariots whirling round at a rapid pace, while the riders held on for dear life as they swayed towards the centre to preserve their equilibrium. Drums and fiddles accompanied the dancers in two or three dancing-tents. Almost every show had its drum, organ, brass-band, gong, or instrument of some sort to bray forth its whereabouts; and those which had not were advertised by the stentorian voice of a show-man or show-woman ceaselessly inviting persons to enter and see the show 'about to begin'. And the shows were various and varied indeed! 'Transparent girls, from Egypt'; fat boys, and fat girls, and fat pigs, and 'rats three feet long'! 'Giant horses', and 'giant lions', and 'giant women'. Men born without arms, and women born without either arms or legs. A sacred ox, 'born with an arm and hand and fingers'. Three tiger-cubs, born eight days before; these belonging to the really good collection of Wombwell's (now Edmond's) menagerie. Then there were marionette shows, and waxwork exhibitions, and indeed it would seem easier to say what there was *not* than to enumerate all that there was. Turning from the exhibitions to the salesmen, Master Cheap-Jack was amongst

ST GILES'S FAIR, BIBLE STALL

the foremost of the latter, offering goods at a shilling and ending by taking a penny; or if that did not succeed, inducing his audience to exchange tenpence for a shilling, and then getting them to spend the shilling so gained in something not worth sixpence! and so on *ad infinitum*.

The special so-called 'fun of the fair' consisted chiefly in sprinkling or besmearing passers-by with coloured brushes, fox-tails, or paper shavings dipped in perfume or dye – a curious repetition of the heathenish custom during the 'Hooli' festival, which is celebrated by the natives of India, by the bedaubing one another with coloured powders and liquids of every hue. Squirts, scratchbacks, and crackers were seemingly prohibited, and the people appeared wonderfully quiet and orderly, bent on earnest amusement, if not on business. The showmen and women and children looked fagged and worn, a sign that their shows had been in good request, and the tinsel and tarlatan of the performing girls' dresses had a crushed and tumbled look, telling of much hard work on their part. Also the wearers had a strangely untrim appearance, as if they were too tired even to smooth the wrinkles in their fleshings, or to pull out the frills and flounces of their skirts. How glad they must all have been when the last bell had rung for the curtain to fall, when the last set of boisterous riders had left the circus, the last hungry lad had devoured his 'one and bread', the last woman had decided on which rattle or doll she would take to her child at home, when the last man had finished his last 'cocoa-nut shy', and the last girl had bought her Brummagem chain for he sweetheart at sea – and last, not least – when they themselves might turn into their green and blue, and yellow, and crimson vans to eat their hardly-earned supper.

Midnight must have struck ere they were thus employed; and soon afterwards nothing would be heard but the low growl of some wild beast of the menagerie, the occasional tramp of the giant horse's hoofs, as he moved uneasily in his

ST GILES'S FAIR, CROWDS

extemporised quarters, or the heavy snore of some stout gipsy, who had been recruiting his strength to the last moment at the nearest tap, which was closed punctually at eleven o'clock by magisterial orders.

Amongst the shows, two had attracted our attention, on account of the quiet respectability of the people concerned in them. One was that of the man born without arms. He told us that at home he worked as a carpenter, and that he had a wife and children whom he thus supported. He could use a hammer or saw with his foot (the left one) as readily and effectually as other men would with their hands. He could open his own door with a latch key, and comb his hair, or write a letter with equal ease. The pen he wielded with his right foot, the toes of which were much smaller than those of the left, which had been used for hard labour. The poor fellow had a good countenance, expressed himself well, and spoke with intelligence. He certainly wrote as well as some people of his class, having the advantage of all their limbs, and better than many.

From this tent we went to see the 'giant horse', which was in charge of a little lad of about fourteen, whose evident pride in the really fine-looking brute, and affection for it, were very pleasant to notice. In answer to our question as to whether it did any work:

'Ay, indeed,' he replied, 'he works *very* hard. He works all day, and draws our heaviest van,' and he patted the creature's shoulder, as high as he could reach it. Its food was slung up 'miles high', as it seemed to us. 'He couldn't reach it no other ways,' as the boy explained; 'and that's not the way to treat a horse,' he interjected reprovingly to some youngsters, who were poking and digging at the patient creature with short sticks. Indeed, it was a true, gentle giant of its kind; and the contrast with a minute very pretty little kitten, curled upon its back for the warmth, was exceedingly curious. The kitten had attached itself to the mighty beast, the boy said, and would not leave it. It rode on the horse's back on the march, and lived on it when at rest; ate, and slept there; and if removed, returned at the first opportunity to its singular friend.

A curious incident occurred on the morning after the fair. At daybreak the work of removal had begun, and by ten o'clock the vans were off the ground, and St Giles' was being rapidly restored to its normal condition of stately picturesqueness by a staff of Local Board men. A few miles outside the town, however, an exciting scene, indirectly

ST GILES'S FAIR, ELECTRIC COLISEUM

connected with the fair, was taking place. A farmer driving to Oxford Market, on the high road near Hampton Poyle, had caught sight of a clumsy-looking shaggy brute in a ditch by a field, busily engaged in devouring a lamb, which seemed to have been snatched from a neighbouring flock. The owner was informed of the strange discovery. Seizing his gun, he hurried to the spot, and despatched the performing bear just as he was in the act of gnawing off the head of the lamb. It seemed a pity to have killed him instead of capturing him to be returned to the proprietor. The bear had a collar round its neck, and, evidently, had escaped from the van *en route* from St Giles' fair to Bicester.

B.B.

THE PRINCE OF WALES

One day, when the Prince of Wales was out with the South Oxfordshire hounds, and sport was not the best, his Royal Highness, with one of his equerries, Colonel Keppel, and two or three undergraduate friends, took a ride across country, and, all unthinkingly, came on to 'Lawyer' H.'s land, finishing up by riding into his farm-yard, with the intent to take a short cut through it. No sooner, however, had the horsemen got into the yard, than H., who was on the watch, had the gate at each end promptly closed and guarded by a party of farm-hands, armed with pitch-forks. Having issued instructions to his force to resist any attempt on the part of the entrapped ones to escape, he saluted the discomfited horsemen with 'Now I've got 'ee!' Asked for an explanation, he announced that he claimed a pound for trespass, and gave all concerned to understand that they would remain where they were till it was forthcoming.

Some one hastened to impart the name of the illustrous personage whom he had impounded, the informant being under the impression that it was only necessary to mention this to ensure an instant release and a humble apology. But 'Lawyer' H. was not built that way, and the only response he vouchsafed was: 'Prince or no prince, I mean to have a sovereign before any of you go.'

His Royal Highness, who was intensely amused when he grasped the situation, took the affront most good-humouredly. As it happened, not anticipating he would ever be called upon to pay ransom in a land over which he was predestined one day to rule, he had made no provision for such an emergency, and had not so much as a sovereign in his pocket. His friends, happily, were able to come to the rescue, and by satisfying the demand in full, secured the release of their future sovereign and themselves.

T.F. Plowman

FULBROOK, FARMYARD

COLLEGES AS LANDLORDS

A considerable portion of the county is owned by the Colleges of Oxford: the traveller will notice how often his inquiries as to the ownership of a farm are met by the answer that it belongs to such and such a college. College property it is true is scattered throughout the length and breadth of England, but, it is naturally more frequent in the parts adjacent to the University. Much of it came from founders and benefactors, but much was also bought by the colleges themselves in the days when land was a profitable investment. Things are otherwise now, but the farmer will still tell you that he would rather hold under a college than under a private landowner; the reason I fear often being that he manages to get more out of the college in the way of improvements.

H.A. Evans

MOTORING

The advent of fine spring weather – has again introduced the great dust fiend. Last Sunday one of the most favourite walks of Witney people, the Burford Road, was rendered quite unusable, owing to the clouds of dust raised by the numerous motor cars passing. Indeed this was the case everywhere along the route of the Oxford and Cheltenham road. – Month after month and year after year, these demons of the roads continue to rush along the highways, raising dust to such an extent as to practically prohibit all other traffic – The authorities must either insist that motors must be constructed in such a manner, and be run at such a pace, as will not raise more dust than ordinary traffic, or they must make the roads in such a manner that no dust can be produced.

Witney Gazette, 20 March 1907

RUSHES ON A PUNT, OXFORD

WILLOWS AND OSIERS

The willow is what scientists and arboriculturists might – and possibly do – style an 'economic' tree; that is to say, it has commercially useful features. Its bark is an excellent medicine for ague, and useful for tanning, although oak-bark is better. The ancient Britons wove their light boats, their 'coracles', from willow-wands, and cricket-bats are now made from its wood. Thus descriptive writers upon cricket-matches, thinking to be picturesque, are frequently found using the vicious phrase 'wielders of the willow', when in fact they mean batsmen. Many varieties of coarse baskets are now manufactured from willow branches. Hence the assiduous pollarding of the willow about once every seventh year, in the middle of winter.

Even the familiar osiers of the Thames have some of these economic uses, and the osiers themselves are a variety of willow.

> By the rushy-fringed bank,
> Where grows the willow and the osier dank,'

says Milton, illustrating, in his *Comus*, the almost inevitable companionship of these leafy cousins.

If we wished most strikingly and picturesquely to describe the difference between an osier and a willow, we should say that an osier was a willow without a trunk. The osiers grow in beds, as a dense array of upright rods, and, to the uninitiated, there is but one kind of osier, but experts are said to be able to distinguish three hundred varieties. Experts are wondrous folk. Strange to say, although we associate osiers with watery flats and soggy patches of ground, the 'hams', or 'holts', as the osier-beds are generally styled, must, if it is desired to grow a good crop, by no means be saturated with water. To successfully form an osier-plantation, the land must be well trenched or otherwise drained of all stagnant or surplus water. Basket-willows refuse to thrive in land that is awash, and they require the sustenance of good manure. Weeds, too, hinder their growth, and they are susceptible to attacks from fly.

All these particulars doubtless come as surprising information to those whose life on the Thames consists merely of rowing, sailing, or camping. If they notice the numerous osier-beds at all, it is only to wonder idly at the dense thickets

BASKET MAKER'S SHOP, CHIPPING NORTON

of tall straight rods they form; and it is but rarely suspected, either that they are carefully planted and tended, or that the crop of rods is both valuable and precarious.

An osier-bed is formed by planting cuttings of some six inches in length. Like cuttings from its big brother, the willow, they strike easily, and soon form vigorous plants. Indeed, in the case of green poles and posts made of willow, many worthy housewives have frequently been astonished at finding the posts they use for hanging out the domestic washing budding lustily and becoming healthy trees.

An osier-rod of one year's growth is ripe for cutting, and cutting proceeds every year, from the established stool: the season's growth being, according to the variety, and to circumstances, anything from ten to fifteen feet.

Osier-growing is a considerable industry, and, with due care and ordinary good fortune, very profitable; for there is not at present a sufficiency grown in England to satisfy the demand, and we thus import largely from France, Belgium, and Holland. But, as shown already, the osier requires to be properly tended, and has its enemies. Prominent among these is the water-rat, whose destructive habits, in gnawing through the base of half-grown rods, are very costly to growers.

The rods are cut in autumn or winter, and are then sorted into four sizes, known as 'Luke', 'Threepenny', 'Middleborough', and 'Great'. Of these, 'Luke' is the smallest. They are done up for sale in 'bolts', i.e. bundles, forty inches round.

To prepare osier-rods for basket-weaving, they are stacked upright in shallow trenches filled with water, their butt-ends immersed from six to eight inches; and thus they are left until spring, when, with the rising of the sap, they begin to throw out buds. When April at last is merging into May, the rods have already burst into leaf and begun forming roots. Then is the opening of the rod-strippers' season; for at this juncture the bark is most easily separated from the rods. Rod-stripping is one of the few surviving primitive rustic industries, carried on, according to the mildness, or otherwise, of the spring, in the open air, or in rustic sheds. This is pre-eminently an occupation for women and children, and generally forms a picturesque scene, not remotely unlike a gipsy encampment. The immemorial instrument used in peeling or stripping the rods is a 'break', formed of two pieces of iron or steel mounted side by side on a wooden post, about waist-high, somewhat resembling an exaggerated tuning-fork, or a 'Jew's harp'. The rods are drawn through the springy embraces of this contrivance, which thus cleanly strips away the bark, and leaves the rod a pure white wand. For the protection of more than usually delicate rods from being bruised, the breaks are occasionally faced with india-rubber.

The whereabouts of a busy group of osier-peelers are readily discovered from some little distance, for the operation of drawing the rods through the breaks is accompanied by a sharp metallic 'ping'; a chorus of these sounds in several keys carrying a long way across the still meadows. And if not by

THE BODLEIAN LIBRARY, OXFORD

sound, certainly by sense of smell is the group of busy workers to be located, for the stripped osiers, or rather, the peelings from them, give forth a strongly aromatic and pungent odour.

The peeled rods are then carefully dried and stored away. They form the material for white baskets, or for baskets that are to be dyed. The rods from the yellow or brown baskets are to be made are treated differently, being peeled in hot water, or in steam; this method – known as 'peeling buff' – bringing out the juices of the rods and staining the surface, according to the variety of osier, buff, brown, or yellow.

Charles G. Harper

THE BODLEIAN

The great Library, in particular, became to me a living and inspiring presence. When I think of it, as it then was, I am aware of a medley of beautiful things – pale sunlight on book-lined walls, or streaming through old armorial bearings on Tudor windows; spaces and distances, all books, beneath a painted roof from which gleamed the motto of the University – *Dominus illuminatio mea*; gowned figures moving silently about the spaces; the faint scents of old leather and polished wood; and fusing it all, a stately dignity and benignant charm, through which the voices of the bells outside, as they struck each successive quarter from Oxford's many towers, seemed to breathe a certain eternal reminder of the past and the dead.

But regions of the Bodleian were open to me then that no ordinary reader sees now. Mr Coxe – the well-known, much-loved Bodley's Librarian of those days – took kindly notice of the girl-reader, and very soon, probably on the recommendation of Mark Pattison, who was a Curator, made me free of the lower floors, where was the 'Spanish room,' with its shelves of seventeenth and eighteenth century volumes in sheepskin or vellum, with their turned-in edges and leathern strings. Here I might wander at will, absolutely alone, save for the visit of an occasional librarian from the upper floor, seeking a book. To get to the Spanish Room one had to pass through the Douce Library, the home of treasures beyond price; on one side half the precious things of Renaissance printing, French or Italian or Elizabethan, on the other, stands of illuminated Missals and Hour Books, many of them rich in pictures and flower-work, that shone like jewels in the golden light of the room. That light was to me something tangible and friendly. It seemed to be the mingled product of all the delicate browns and yellows and golds in the bindings of the books, of the brass lattice work that covered them, and of reflections from the beautiful stone-work of the Schools Quadrangle outside. It was in these noble surroundings that, with far too little, I fear, of positive reading, and with much undisciplined wandering from shelf to shelf and subject to subject, there yet sank deep into me the sense of history, and of that vast ocean of the recorded past, from which the generations rise, and into which they fall back. And that in itself was a great boon – almost, one might say, a training, of a kind.

Mrs Humphry Ward

RAILWAY STATION, CHIPPING NORTON

FINDING YOUR WAY

A few days ago a stranger alighted at the railway station [Chipping Norton], and journeying up New Street paused to enquire his way. Seeing presumably an old inhabitant he asked if he could direct him to Mr —, naming a well-known local man. 'Oh yes, sir', replied the veteran, 'you can't miss it, it's almost in a straight line after you leave the Market Place. Go up Pembroke Street and take the first opening on your right through Giles' Yard, this brings you into Back Lane, turn to the left and the first turn on the right is Windmill Lane; the gentleman lives right at the top of that.' 'Thank you, my friend', said the stranger, 'and as I am in a hurry to catch a train I will write down the return route, the nearest way, I mean, to the station.' 'Well, sir', replied the native, 'when you come down Windmill Lane you will see a public-house called the Three Tuns, turn round by Ward's Corner. Anyone will show you, and you come to Tite End, first turn on the right is Clay Lane, and through the churchyard and by way of Diston's Lane, and you are straight for the station.'

About four hours later a worn-out looking man entered the booking office again and met the same obliging porter who had taken charge of his bag. 'Hope you found the gentleman all right, sir' said the official, with an eye to a tip. 'Found him! Confound it, no. Pembroke Street had gone, no one had ever heard of it; Giles' Yard was Portland Place; Back Lane, Albion Street; Windmill Lane, Rock Hill; why, even the wretched pub was called by another name, and when I asked for the Tite End, people thought me mad, and said that was Spring Street. Clay Lane, after a struggle, I found to be Church Lane, and Diston's Lane was King Edward Street. I forgot to say that when I did get to the top of Windmill Lane the man had left, but as I was afraid his new street had probably changed its name also, I gave it up. Bless it!'

Oxfordshire Weekly News, 14 October 1908

DUCKLINGTON

An Outing to Ducklington

The North Oxfordshire Archaeological Society met on the first of August last, and excursionized to Bampton, by Ducklington, Cokethorpe, Stanlake, and Yelford. The party and weather were in good humour, and kept to it during the day. The former soon found themselves at Ducklington, a mile and a quarter from Witney, and could not but be struck with the breadth of rurality there stretched before them, in the large village green – in the spread out pond, in the roomy rectory, with lawns, and tall trees, and flickering shadows, and in that – centering and completing the whole – the church. Here, said one of the party, come teams and cows to the water, ducks and geese remaining all day. The labourers pass it in the morning and return to it with the sun-set. Here old and young from time to time gather – talking, laughing, singing. Here on holidays the crowd thickens and the fun waxes louder. Then again, on those adjoining lawns and under those elms are children, and in that house of many chambers the parson, who works hard as any of his parishioners in the fields. And once more, what a picture opens upon us, the Sunday groups by twos and threes, gathering to church or returning from prayer, to happy talk at home. We may as well, said he, let our eyes drink in these scenes, just as we do well to note the buildings of past days and their contents and surroundings, for the *lex equilibrii* has been disturbed, not only on the continent but in our own land, and we are (as a nation) at this moment more progressive than permanent.

Transactions of the North Oxfordshire Archaeological Society (1871)

Chalgrove: A Sketch

'Far from the Madding Crowd' is a very true description of our village for we are four good miles from the nearest market town, a sleepy little place, quietly pursuing 'the even tenor of its way'.

I suppose a stranger would see little difference between Chalgrove and many other English villages. It consists of one street. The road runs with a slight curve for some distance, and then branches off to the right and left. At this point is 'a spreading chestnut tree', and, not under it but close by, is the village smithy, with the somewhat curious inscription over the door, 'M. Brown, black and white smith'. On either side of the road are cottages and barns, built with small regard to regularity, with a break here and there of pasture or arable land. The cottages are, many of them, very old and sadly dilapidated, but just the sort of 'subjects' that look so picturesque in an artist's sketchbook, with their thatched and sloping roofs and whitewashed walls. Each cottage has its piece of garden ground, and a good deal of money is sometimes earned in prizes given at the horticultural show, which is held every year at the neighbouring town. The Vicarage is almost the only house of any pretension, though some of the farm homesteads are picturesque and rambling old buildings, the relics of former grandeur, when the village boasted its hall and manor. The remains of the moat which once surrounded the manor house are still to be seen. A little farther on is the green, where stood the stocks and the cross; but, alas! the stones of which the cross was built are now scattered through the village, and sadly diverted from their original use – the

CHALGROVE

foundation-stone forming the basin of a pump, and another serving for a stile.

A brook, bordered with old trees, runs through the village, so that on one side the cottages are approached by bridges, or more often by merely a rough plank. This brook is a branch of another stream, which takes a parallel course through fields and meadows and turns the mill. In rainy seasons these overflow, and the road, for a time, resembles a river, when numerous are the expedients for getting about, to which we have to resort. Every boy, who can manage it, has a pair of stilts, on which he is almost as much at home as on his own legs, while to the children it is nearly as good as a seaside outing. During the spell of severe weather in January, 1881, we were quite blockaded for nearly a week; provisions began to run short, and as for the post, that was quite out of the question, so that for a time we seemed out of the world. After the heavy snowstorms we were as usual deeply flooded, and instead of the road there was a broad and rapid stream. In the night the water froze, and from one end of the village to the other the road was covered with a sheet of thick rough ice, rendering any locomotion, except on skates, almost impossible. Gangs of men, who reaped quite a harvest out of

FLOODS, THAME

THE FERRY, BABLOCK HYTHE

the ice and snow, were of course speedily set to work to clear the roads, but it was a long time before the last remnant of ice disappeared.

Chalgrove Church stands in the fields, and very picturesque are the glimpses that one gets of it between the trees. It is a large and ancient structure, in the Norman style, and dedicated to St. Mary. During a violent tempest, in the year 1727, the steeple fell to the ground. It was replaced by a massive battlemented tower. The chancel is private property; it is of very ordinary appearance, but contains sedilia and a piscina of a somewhat uncommon type, and also brasses bearing the date of the thirteenth century. In 1858, the whitewash on the walls having been removed, they were found to be covered with a series of frescoes, dating from the thirteenth and fourteenth centuries. In a paper on these paintings communicated to the Society of Antiquaries by William Burges, Esq., he says: 'These very curious paintings are some of the most perfect, if not the most perfect, we have remaining in this country. The chancel of Chalgrove Church is probably the only place where an idea can be formed of the general effect of the more humble class of paintings of the thirteenth and fourteenth centuries.'

The church boasts a fine peal of six bells, not to be equalled, in our opinion at least, for many miles round. The little 'ting-tang' is the most ancient, and bears the date of 1659. When the tower was rebuilt two bells were added; one of them, the tenor, bears the inscription:

> To the Church the living do call,
> And to the grave do summon all.

The Pelican

BABLOCK HYTHE

Sweet-named Bablock Hythe is 11 miles by water from Folly Bridge, but only 4 by road. Its rope ferry is the only one now remaining on the Thames of these once frequent worries. The line hangs at times a bare 2 feet or less above the water, and is heavy and rigid withal; so that unless you manage your approach carefully it will rap your head pretty shrewdly. The river here is broad and deep; and the whole 2 miles from Skinner's weir very charming.

F.S. Thacker

RADCLIFFE INFIRMARY, OXFORD

Henry Acland: A Memoir

Acland's first introduction to municipal life dated from his appointment as Lee's Reader in Anatomy, when he found himself officially required to be a Commissioner of Lighting and Paving. What the state of affairs was at that time and for years after, under the rule of the city authorities, has appeared sufficiently in the story of the cholera outbreak. Acland has summed it up in another place in vigorous language:

> The sanitary condition of Oxford and its surroundings was deplorable. The workhouse was ill-placed and ill-managed; human *excreta* which entered the river from the lowest parts of the suburbs were pumped unfiltered through the town. The alleys were miserable. There was no attempt at protecting the Thames from the sewage, such as there was, of the houses; the Commissioners had no adequate power to raise money on loan so as to remedy systematically the frightful evils. Such was the force of custom and aversion to change that when it was proposed to abolish the Paving Acts, as they were called, and to place the town under the improved Imperial Laws, the motion was not even seconded, though at a subsequent meeting of the Commissioners it was carried by ten to one.

In a speech, delivered at a dinner of the Oxford Corporation in 1892, Acland was able to point to a veritable revolution along the whole line. A new Union House had been built, the Thames had been purified of its turbid filth, a system of drainage had been constructed in accordance with the most modern requirements and in conjunction with a sewage farm. A new and constant water-supply was served from admirably equipped waterworks, and the arrangements for the care of the masses in sickness had been altered out of all recognition. The Radcliffe Infirmary had been extended and improved in every direction, a hospital for infectious diseases had been constructed, a competent officer of health appointed, and a complete system of nursing the sick – poor and rich alike – had been established. With regard to all these great changes Acland was well entitled to say *pars magna fui*. As a member of the Board of Guardians and the Board of Health he had been persistent and untiring, as Physician to the

FLOODS IN LAKE STREET, OXFORD

Radcliffe he had, in the face of much opposition, active and passive, carried most necessary reforms, and his practical knowledge of sanitation had always been at the service of the Corporation with regard to drainage and water-supply. He took a leading part in abolishing the old pauperizing doles, in obtaining a new Charity Scheme, and in organizing out of the old Cutler Boulter Foundation a new Provident Dispensary, through which the working-classes were visited and treated in their own homes.

Much of this work, during the earlier stages at any rate, was done in the face of great discouragement. 'The longer I live here,' he wrote in 1866, 'the more unbearable it seems to me. The Dean and I have both been pointedly told that whatever he or I proposed at the Local Board would have been equally and violently opposed.' The vested interests and the forces of ignorance and prejudice would have been too strong for Acland, even with Liddell to help him, but for the fact that earnest and enlightened men were gradually replacing the Do-nothings and the busybodies both in the City and the University: the difficult thing was to organize them and to promote harmonious working between townsman and gownsman.

Here was Acland's great opportunity. In his two-fold capacity of Physician and Professor he belonged to both parties. The antagonism between the Corporation and the University authorities was traditional and apparently irremediable. As late as 1858 we find the Mayor of Oxford declining to take the oath to observe the privileges of the University, and Convocation first authorizing the Vice-Chancellor to proceed against that official with all the rigours of the law, and then empowering him to abstain from opposing the Bill intended to relieve the Mayor (Mr Isaac Grubb) from the obligation to which he had conceived an objection. The causes of the antagonism lay deep down in academical history. To-day it is almost a thing of the past; the University is represented in every municipal institution, it contributes its quota of members to the Town Council, and its most distinguished sons do not shrink from their share in the government of the city. In this great process of union and reconciliation, culminating in the Act of 1889, Acland was the pioneer. He threw himself vigorously into all that concerned the health and welfare of Oxford, he attended meetings, served on committees, gave lectures, was insistent – in season and out of season – in preaching his unpopular gospel of cleanliness and sanitation. On the Local Board he, and Rolleston after him, discharged without remuneration the duties of a permanent Health Officer. Nor was he neglectful of purely social agencies. In evening parties at his own house, in more ceremonial soirées at the Radcliffe Camera and the New Museum, he knew no distinction between town and gown. The progressive and public-spirited element among the Oxford tradesfolk were brought face to face with all the punctilious elements in academical society. By degrees the barriers were broken down. Other Dons beside Liddell and Acland and Neate were found to interest themselves in the details of civic work. Rolleston and Thorold Rogers, and in a later generation T.H. Green and Humphry Ward, followed in

RADCLIFFE HOSPITAL, OXFORD

the same path. But no member of the University ever came to occupy the position in the estimation and affection of the townsfolk which Acland ultimately filled. During the later years of his life his influence was supreme; his tact, his urbanity, his commanding presence, and the remembrance of his self-denying life and his services in the past, placed him without a rival in the hearts of his fellow citizens.

J.B. Atlay

PRECIOUS WATER

Against the wall of every well-kept cottage stood a tarred or green-painted water butt to catch and store the rain-water from the roof. This saved many journeys to the well with buckets, as it could be used for cleaning and washing clothes and for watering small, precious things in the garden. It was also valued for toilet purposes and the women would hoard the last drops for themselves and their children to wash in. Rain-water was supposed to be good for the complexion, and, though they had no money to spend upon beautifying themselves, they were not too far gone in poverty to neglect such means as they had to that end.

For drinking water, and for cleaning water, too, when the water butts failed, the women went to the well in all weathers, drawing up the buckets with a windlass and carting them home suspended from their shoulders by a yoke . . .

In dry summers, when the hamlet wells failed, water had to be fetched from a pump at some farm buildings half a mile distant. Those who had wells in their gardens would not give away a spot, as they feared if they did theirs, too, would run dry, so they fastened down the lids with padlocks and disregarded all hints.

Flora Thompson

EARLY MOTORING

Plea for a Speed Limit

It is quite time that motor machines should be compelled to obey the law with regard to the speed they run through our streets. It is no uncommon thing to see these machines running at something over 20 miles an hour, and unless the mad-capped drivers are stopped, some serious accident is sure to occur sooner or later – They should certainly be prohibited from running after lighting up time. They are quite bad enough to meet in broad daylight, but at night they are perfect demons.

Witney Gazette, 26 April 1900

Ploughing

Now, the two-wheeled plough, made of iron with steel mould-board and drawn by two horses, is in common use, though on the clay soils three horses are often required. On the light soils, double-furrow ploughs, drawn by three horses abreast, are becoming more numerous every year, and are a great saving of horse labour. Special-purpose ploughs, such as the ridging plough, the digging plough, and the potato-raising plough, are also in use. Ploughing is now universally done by horse and steam power. During the middle of the last century and up to recent years bullocks were worked on the land, but scarcely a team of these animals can now be found.

PLOUGH TEAM, SARSDEN CROSS

V.C.H. Oxon.

HIRING FAIR, BURFORD

BURFORD HIRING FAIR

So, from my window I watch the manners of the present age, and note that it is exactly 8 o'clock by the Witney hooter when the first men for hire pass along. Strong, sturdy fellows, dressed better than I can afford to. No smock frocks nowadays! soon others come, for the most part on bicycles, and women are coming, too in traps. No walking five miles or so in these luxurious days! . . . A serious day it is for these people. Today is to decide where the coming year shall be spent. Serious or not, no one looks it. They pass me down the Hill with a cheery 'good morning' and go down to the Fair, first stopping to get the time honoured drink, either at the 'White Horse', the 'Swan', or the 'New Inn'. Many, and many a man, who shall go down the Burford Hill today, has never broken the custom, it may be through a long lifetime! . . . Every year the Fair seems to get more and more orderly, indeed this time I was struck with the extreme respectability of everything.

Witney Gazette, 28 September 1907

SOCIAL LIFE

For six months of the year Oxford is a city of young men, for the most part between the ages of eighteen and twenty-two. In my maiden days it was not also a city of young women, as it is to-day. Women – girls especially – were comparatively on sufferance. The Heads of Houses were married; the Professors were mostly married; but married tutors had scarcely begun to be. Only at two seasons of the year was Oxford invaded by women – by bevies of maidens who came, in early May and middle June, to be made much of by their brothers and their brothers' friends, to be danced with and flirted with, to know the joys of coming back on a summer night from Nuneham up the long fragrant reaches of the lower river, or of 'sitting out' in historic gardens where Philip Sidney or Charles I had passed.

At the Eights and 'Commem.' the old, old place became a mere background for pretty dresses, and college luncheons, and river picnics. The seniors groaned often, as well they might; for there was little work done in my day in the summer term. But it is perhaps worth while for any nation to possess

STUDENTS AT WORCESTER COLLEGE, OXFORD

such harmless festivals in so beautiful a setting as these Oxford gatherings. How many of our national festivals are spoilt by ugly and sordid things – betting and drink, greed and display! Here, all there is to see is a competition of boats, manned by England's best youth, upon a noble river, flowing, in Virgilian phrase, 'under ancient walls'; a city of romance given up for a few days to the pleasure of the young, and breathing into that pleasure her own refining, exalting note; a stately ceremony – the Encaenia – going back to the infancy of English learning; and the dancing of young men and maidens in Gothic or classical halls built long ago by the 'fathers who begat us.' My own recollection of the Oxford summer, the Oxford river and hayfields, the dawn on Oxford streets, as one came out from a Commemoration ball, or the evening under Nuneham woods where the swans on that still water, now, as always, 'float double, swan and shadow' – these things I hope will be with me to the end. To have lived through them is to have tasted youth and pleasure from a cup as pure, as little alloyed with baser things, as the high gods allow to mortals.

Mrs Humphry Ward

Witney Blankets

We draw our supplies of wool from various sources. Of course we use largely English wool – both 'fleece wool', shorn of the live sheep, and 'skin wool', taken by the fellmonger off the skins of sheep killed by the butcher; we also used English wool in the form of 'noils', which is the shorter staple left after the long wool has been combed for the purpose of spinning worsted. We also use wools from Australia, New Zealand, East India, and other wool-producing countries.

The first process is the blending of the various sorts of wool, for we seldom or never make a blanket out of one sort of wool alone, but several kinds are brought together in a blend, each one being intended to affect the whole according to its own special characteristics. And here, of course, our long experience and carefully kept records are of the greatest value.

The wool is then put through the Willey, or 'Willow' (probably so called from being originally made as a cylinder of basket work), for the purpose of preparing it for the carding machines. First comes the Shake Willey, which is a machine running at a high speed, the cylinders of which are fitted with

WILLEYING THE WOOL, WITNEY

iron spikes to beat and roughly open the wool, the dust from which is carried away by a fan. The second willeying machine, the 'Teazer', has its cylinders closely set with small curved steel teeth, which further open the wool, and at this stage it is automatically sprinkled with a fine spray of oil, which is intended to prevent the staple being broken in the carding process, and to lubricate the fibres and cause them readily to lend themselves to the spinning process.

From the Willey room the wool is taken to the carding machines, consisting of a 'Scribbler' and 'Carder'. They are both composed of large cylinders by which the wool is conveyed from one end of the machine to the other. Above these large cylinders are placed smaller rollers to intercept and open any hard knots of wool and to assist in thoroughly mixing the various fibres; space is also left by which particles of dirt fall under the machine. All the rollers of these machines are covered with 'cards', or sheets of leather or rubber cloth stuck full of bent steel wires; these manipulate the fibre, like tens of thousands of minute fingers, and are graduated from coarse and strong at the commencement to fine and delicate wires at the finish of the process. In passing through these machines the wool is first put into the hopper of an automatic feeding machine, which, with the greatest delicacy, weighs and delivers on to the feed sheet of the Scribbler the required quantity of wool, and as we watch the steady motion of this machine it is hard to believe that *brains* are not to be found in some part of its structure.

When the wool has passed through the Scribbler it is removed from the last roller by a very rapidly moving steel blade, and is delivered in a continuous sheet to a feeding machine, by which it is placed on the feed sheet of the Carder, through which it also passes. The last roller of the Carder is covered with rings of 'card' by which the sheet of wool issuing from the machine is divided into loosely formed 'slivers', and these, after passing between leather rubbers to give them some consistence, are wound on to long wooden bobbins like great cotton reels.

These bobbins are placed in a row along the back of the Spinning Mule, and here the threads are stretched to the right size. They have the necessary amount of twist given to them, and are wound on to wooden spools, ready to be placed in the weaver's shuttle. This Spinning Mule, or Self-actor as it is termed, is a triumph of mechanical invention and construction, though we must remember that the smoothly

WEIGHING IMPORTED WOOL, WITNEY

SHEEP SHEARING

The most ancient of the manufacturing arts

THE LOOM SHED, WITNEY

working, almost thoughtful, machine as we see it to-day, was not the product of one brilliant invention, but the result of much experience and many improvements.

We next proceed to the Power Loom Weaving Shed, and amid the clash and din of many looms watch the modern form of the most ancient of the manufacturing arts.

Most of our looms are of the simple character used for the weaving of ordinary blankets, but we have also a number of Jacquard looms on which we weave runs of elaborate figured designs, such as are in demand for the South American and South African markets.

The woven piece when cut from the loom has the appearance of a roll of canvas or sacking, very different from the spotless fleecy article known as a Witney Blanket. The only suggestion that it is a piece of blanket arises from the coloured stripes which have been woven in with fast-dyed yarns, and which mark the top and bottom of each blanket when the piece is finished and cut up.

This material, of such unpromising appearance, is dirty and greasy and requires cleansing; it is also too loose and open, and requires shrinking up to the proper thickness. To see these processes carried out we now proceed to the 'Stock House'.

On our way thither we can visit the Dyeing Department, which we find thoroughly equipped with machinery and cisterns for scouring and dyeing piece goods, and the wool and yarns used in the headings of the blankets, and in the rugs of which we make large quantities for the Home and Foreign Markets.

Arriving at the Stock House we see that the piece is first passed through an alkaline solution, and then put into the Fulling Stocks, where it is pounded and beaten by the heavy hammers or feet, a process which not only shrinks the fabric, but causes the alkali to combine with the grease in the cloth, forming suds which are afterwards thoroughly rinsed out in a washing machine, leaving the piece perfectly clean. It is now passed through a bath of soap and put back into the Fulling Stocks or into the Milling Machine, in either case to be subjected to pressure and friction, which complete the shrinking process, and leave the cloth of the right substance.

After a final wash, to brighten the colour, the piece is placed in a Centrifugal Machine, and spun round about 1,000 times a minute; this throws off most of the water, and leaves the piece dry enough for the bleaching process.

Our special make of old-fashioned unbleached goods have

SHEEP DIPPING, RADCOT BRIDGE

EMPLOYEES, WITNEY MILL

no alkali or soap put upon them, and of course do not undergo the bleaching process; they are simply cleansed with fuller's-earth, are wet-raised, and then are dried in the sun and air, which are the only bleaching agents brought to bear upon them.

But the demand for smart appearance makes the frequent mistake of sacrificing somewhat of intrinsic value for the sake of pleasing the eye, so that the pieces of ordinary goods are taken from the Stock House and hung up in the Bleach House, which is a chamber as nearly air-tight as possible, sulphur is lighted, and the goods hang exposed to the fumes for about 10 hours. This process whitens them, but at the same time gives the harmless, but sometimes rather pungent, smell that usually arises from new blankets of the ordinary make. The unbleached goods are of course entirely free from this smell.

When taken from the Bleach House the pieces are stretched on the tenters to dry – out of doors in fine weather, and in long steam-heated chambers in wet weather. We avail ourselves of the clear condition of our atmosphere by having many ranges of out-door tenters, and in suitable weather we daily dry more than a mile of blankets at a time in this way.

Our piece, though now clean, dry and white, is yet a hard, heavy fabric; it has none of the soft fleecy character that makes a Witney Blanket such a splendid non-conductor of heat, and enables those who sleep under it to realise what is meant by

Warmth without weight

WHIPPING THE EDGES, WITNEY

DISPATCHING THE WOOL, WITNEY

CRAWLEY MILL

warmth without weight. Our friends looking at a piece in this stage frequently ask: 'But how do you put the wool on?' We do not put it on, we draw it out of the fabric. This is done by passing the piece under a revolving cylinder clothed with a spiral of wire card, the teeth of which draw out the fibres of wool from the surface of the cloth. After passing through this machine, every piece is carefully finished by hand.

The unbleached wet-raised goods are passed through a somewhat similar machine, but the raising surface instead of being wire card consists of Teazle heads, the strong hooked teeth of which answer the same purpose.

The piece is now cut up into single blankets, the edges of each are whipped with worsted or bound with silk, and every blanket is once more carefully scrutinised, and finally smoothed over ready for packing. Thus at last, after a bewildering series of processes, we have succeeded in producing that which can be produced nowhere else in this wide world, a 'REAL WITNEY BLANKET'.

Anon.

THE GARLAND

Charlton-on-Otmoor. The church is dedicated in the name of St Mary the Virgin. Feast Sunday is the next Sunday after September 19th, and should this be a Sunday, the 26th is Feast Sunday. This is often called 'Great Feast Sunday', as so many churches dedicated to the B.V.M. have their feast at this time. The Nativity of the Virgin, on September 8th, is the festival which fixes this date. A fair takes place on the Monday following Feast Sunday.

At Charlton-on-Otmoor the large cross made of wood, with a circular base which stands on the rood-screen, is known locally as 'The Garland'. It is completely covered with spring flowers and evergreens, and placed on the screen on the first of May. The old woman who has lately superintended the dressing of 'The Garland', speaks of it as 'My Lady', talks about 'giving her a waist', and calls the flowers down the front 'buttons'. The arms of the cross are 'her arms'. In earlier days there used to be two crosses, a larger and a smaller one. The two crosses were carried about bedecked with flowers, the larger by the men, the smaller

SCHOOLCHILDREN, WESTON-ON-THE-GREEN

by the women, but this custom has fallen into disuse. At such times the Cross would be set down at the corner of the Churchyard, and the morris-dancers would dance up and down before it. The Garland is now dressed, and placed on the screen on May Day. Children sometimes carry about little crosses decked with flowers and sing a May Day song, but compulsory school attendance has nearly put an end to the custom. There are people living who can remember the great cross being carried over Otmoor to Studley Priory, where Lady Croke used to give the party 10s. It was accompanied by the morris-dancers. Young married women remember as girls carrying the smaller cross round the village. Old morris-dancers are still living, and describe the small bells that were fastened on their leather leggings. An old man remembers to have danced after his marriage in 1858, but 'there was not much going about then'. He thinks it died out about 1863.

Oxfordshire Archaeological Society, 1903

LADYSMITH

There was a lively scene when we suddenly received the news of the relief of Ladysmith. The whole City went mad. No preparations had been made for bonfires, so hoardings and scaffoldings were torn down, tables, chairs and sofas were hurled from windows and huge bonfires were lighted in the streets. It was a downright merry night. The climax to the destruction of personal property seemed to be reached when I watched a piano being thrown from a window in The Broad. No one who did not live through the tension of the days of that siege can appreciate the relief that we all felt. Gone was the time of suspense, of Colenso and Spion Kop. Once more it would be said that we had never lost a siege. No wonder that both young and old Oxford went mad. In my recollection of forty years it has never done the like again.

H.E. Counsell

POSTMEN, STEEPLE ASTON

The Postman

Tom Phipps, the postman. I can see him now – fresh, hearty, jaunty, swinging along with an easy but rather short step, and bidding you good-day in a high cheery musical voice. He walked some three-and-twenty miles every week-day, besides working in a garden in the early afternoon, and was just as brisk at the end of his day as at the beginning. The walking did not weary him because his eyes and mind were ever on the alert. It was a treat to hear him, in his old age, tell of birds and animals he had noticed in his walks, and if anyone ever writes a book on the Fauna of Oxfordshire, he may be glad to know of Tom's positive assertion that he had once seen a 'marten-cat' in Bruern Wood. He was, of course, perfectly happy in all weathers, and in the great snow-storm of January 18, 1881, he was the only postman in the district who struggled through it and entirely carried out his duty.

Tom was an exceptionally vigorous man, and came, I should say, of a vigorous family of middle-sized men with black curly hair, a rare thing, this last, in our parts. He had a large family himself, and he was one of a large family too, for he used to tell how his father, when the tenth child made his appearance, took him to old Parson Western and offered him as a tithe of his family. This was in the days before the Tithes Commutation Act, and Tom's father did not see why if the parson relieved him of his tenth sheaf and his tenth egg, he should not also relieve him of his tenth baby.

W.W. Fowler

University Police

The actual police duties were taken in alternate weeks by the senior and the junior proctor.

I was troubled by one most vexatious incident in the middle of the Christmas vacation, the theft from the Bodleian of a valuable book. The culprit was never discovered, but, as careful investigations proved, was probably one of two individuals. But the methods of Sherlock Holmes were not within the power of the proctorial staff, who could not disguise themselves as gas inspectors or touting agents, in order to get entrance into a private house: and it so chanced that neither of our suspects was living in College or in licensed lodgings.

HIGH STREET, OXFORD

Each proctor had two assistants, the pro-proctors nominated by himself. They took over, during the week for which the proctor was responsible, four of the obligatory night-promenades so familiar to the public of the highways, while their chief was responsible for the other three; he of course chose the evenings when any trouble might be expected – such as the 5th of November – always lively with fireworks and even as late as 1894 liable to be diversified by 'town and gown rows' – though they were beginning to go out of fashion. There was also a certain expectation of mischief when there happened to be a parliamentary election in progress, or when some abnormal political meeting was announced.

With the proctor or the pro-proctor on duty for the night there always marched the rank and file of the university police, the 'Marshal', their non-commissioned officer, and two or sometimes three of the 'bull-dogs', as undergraduates called them. The Marshal was a most intelligent person, for long years a sergeant in the Oxfordshire Light Infantry, and very much the old soldier. I had many an amusing conversation with him, when business was slack and streets were empty during our nocturnal rambles. The bull-dogs were all middle-aged or elderly men, not chosen for their powers of running, but for their encyclopaedic knowledge of undergraduate personalities. Within a few weeks of the beginning of the Academic year they had usually obtained a very fair idea as to which of the freshmen were sly or noisy boys, while among the second and third year men they had a marvellous acquaintance with our usually very genial and amusing 'criminal classes'. Of course they did not know the abnormal catches of the proctorial net – quiet and harmless undergraduates who fell by mere chance into our purview, while on their legitimate errands but capless and gownless. I used to pass the studious youth with books under his arm, or the dusty 'hiker' returning from a long evening walk with a nod and a caution.

The Marshal and the senior bull-dog had both of them extraordinary capacities of long sight: while we were fifty yards away they would warn me 'members of the A club going home in liquor', or 'Mr. B. of C. College clinging to a post', or 'Mr. D. going along breaking gas-lamps again', or occasionally 'a member and a "character" down that dark entry'. If a fleet-footed suspect absconded, he was not generally followed, for the chances were that he was known by sight to one of the proctorial band; if not, he could certainly have outrun a pursuer of forty-five years of age. The individuals with whom I had to deal were generally *not* in a condition to use their heels to any great effect. The bull-dogs, besides their wonderful acquaintance with the junior academic public had also a sight-knowledge of certain undesirable town-dwellers of both sexes, 'bookies', 'touts', and light ladies who occasionally came under our notice.

Five-sixths of the 140 cases with which I had to deal in my year were trivial and often amusing breaches of the academic

BROAD STREET, OXFORD

by-laws, for which fixed penalties were provided in the printed code passed on from proctor to proctor. Such were 'smoking in academicals' – worth 5s. in 1894 but now an obsolete offence – making loud noises in the streets, playing billiards in public rooms after 10 p.m., giving dinners in hotels to large parties of friends without having first obtained official leave, haunting tap-rooms with obvious signs of the visit when discovered, climbing up buildings or monuments without harm done, or running away with advertisement boards and replacing them in inappropriate spots. I had many a laugh with the criminals on the morning after the offence and they left little money behind.

Of all my interviews with these genial offenders, the most amusing was one on the 5th of November 1894. The spire of St Mary's Church was under repairs, and its gallery was accessible by a series of long ladders. The Marshal pointed out to me a figure far aloft. I shouted up to the climber a recommendation to come down. He replied with an intimation that he could stop up there as long as he pleased, and that the bull-dogs would not like the climb. To this I made a practical retort by ordering my staff to remove the lowest of the ladders, and then reminded my interlocutor that he could not get down, and would have to stop in his lofty and rather chilly perch all night, unless we came to an agreement. He saw the practical wisdom of compromise, and the ladder was replaced. When we resumed conversation on *terra firma* he explained to me that he had gone up to get a bird's eye view of the many bonfires which were blazing in College quadrangles on Guy Fawkes' night. I agreed that the idea was inspiring, but objected that dangerous ascents of University buildings by night were against the rules. However, I rather admired his initiative, and assured him that no great fuss would be made when he came to the proctor's room at 10 a.m. on November 6th. When he presented himself I had to fine him a sovereign – a modest penalty: this coin having been passed over, he (to my surprise) produced a number of other coins – Anglo-Saxon pennies just dug up on his uncle's estate, and asked me to identify them – which I did. We had a pleasant archaeological chat, and parted good friends. He is still alive – a very distinguished and prominent personage – we have met several times in later years, and laughed over the incident. I had always a weakness for the climbers of the 'Oxford Alpine Club' to which at least one future Cabinet Minister belonged.

On two occasions I had to deal with climbers in much more unpleasant situations than my friend on St Mary's spire. One unfortunate had endeavoured to get over the revolving spikes above the iron gate between Corpus and Merton.

ASTHALL

While he was straddling them, they gave a twist, and he was caught with clothes perforated by several spikes, and with one at least impinging in a soft part of his person. Unable to move without danger of further bodily damage, he gave tongue loudly – and attracted in a moment the attention both of a policeman and of the proctor and staff, who happened to be passing through Oriel Street. He had to be got down with the aid of a ladder – his bodily punishment was already, I considered, almost sufficient, and he got off very lightly. The other case was that of a ne'er-do-well who had been 'sent down', but had returned surreptitiously to Oxford: he was caught three-quarters of the way up a rope, which had been let down to him by a friend living in a second storey in lodgings. Just as he was nearing his destination, the Marshal spied him, hauled on the rope, and shook him down, supposing him to be a burglar. When brought to the ground he proved to be merely some one who ought to have been in London in disgrace. He was sent back there after being mulcted with a fine, which he had great difficulty in paying, as his return to Oxford had been with the object of borrowing money from acquaintances. This was his last visit to the University, which was well rid of him.

Sir Charles Oman

AGRICULTURAL WAGES

With regard to the hiring of agricultural labour, the custom of Oxfordshire varies very much from that of, say, the East Riding of Yorkshire. In the latter young farm hands are hired for the year and boarded in the hirer's house, but there is no such custom in Oxfordshire, where the labourers receive from 12*s*. to 14*s*. a week, and cowmen, shepherds, and horsemen, who work seven days a week, generally have their cottages rent-free. They have some potato land found for them on the farm, and at harvest take the harvest work at so much an acre to cut, generally carrying corn and stacking it by contract. This custom only holds good on large farms. Where the holdings are small extra allowance is made for beer and extra wages paid for overtime. The general hours of work are from 7 a.m. to 5 p.m., with an hour off for dinner. The wages are low, the cottages often very miserable, and the general aspect of the labourer inferior to that of the north country farm hand. . . . Oxfordshire agriculture suffers from the same cause that has considerably reduced all farming profits in other counties, namely, the cost of distribution, for it frequently costs about half as much to put the article on the market as to produce it.

V.C.H. Oxon.

CHILDREN PADDLING, COWLEY

WITNEY INFANT SCHOOL

>This is the Witney Infant School,
>Where we are taught the happy rule,
>To love our God and parents kind,
>And leave all useless things behind.
>But we must come with faces clean,
>Neat clothes, all whole, fit to be seen:
>And only a penny do we pay
>Per week for learning every day.
>Then let us all attend to time,
>Be there before, or just at *nine*;
>And in the afternoon so true
>Be always in the School at two.
>Now we will all attention pay
>To all that our kind teachers say;
>And pray that God may bless our school,
>Its friends, and every infant rule.

Anon.

A TRIP ON THE RIVER

The day we left Streatley, the hot August sun had come at last. It was warm and close in the village, warm and fresh on the water. The *Golden Grasshopper*, the famous yellow and white houseboat of the last Henley Regatta, had just anchored near 'The Swan', and its proprietor was tacking up awnings and renewing his flower frieze, which sadly needed the attention, but he monopolized the energy of the river. Boats lay at rest under the railway bridge below Streatley and under the trees of Hart's Woods.

In riverside gardens children practised what Mr Ashby-Sterry calls 'hammockuity'. Anglers dozed in the sun. The only living creature who seemed awake was a vulgar little boy who, when we passed a sheepwash in a pretty backwater and asked him when the sheep were washed, told us, 'Why when it's toime, of coorse'.

'O, Pangbourn is pleasant in sweet summer time', with its old wooden bridge to Whitchurch over the river, and the lock with delicate birches on its island, and the mill and the weir

WHITCHURCH BRIDGE

and the gables and red roofs and tall elms. In all Thames villages the elements of picturesqueness are the same; in each they come together with new beauty. We had scarce left Pangbourn before we passed Hardwick House, red, gabled, and Elizabethan, and the more impressive because, as a rule, the big private houses on the Thames are ugly. And not far beyond was Mapledurham Mill, a fair rival to Iffley, and Mapledurham Lock, which many people, beside Dick in Mr Morris' *Utopia*, 'think a very pretty place'; and on the other side of the lock Mapledurham House, of whose beauty every one tells you. But you cannot see it from the river, and its owner will not let you land. His shores are barricaded by the sign 'Private'; there is no inn in the village; he has but lately asked the courts to forbid fishermen to throw their lines in the Thames, as it flows past his estate; and the only wonder is that he has not hung up a curtain in front of the beautiful trees that line his river bank.

J. & E. Robins Pennell

MAPLEDURHAM MILL

TEA PARTY, SOMERVILLE COLLEGE

Women Students

The woman student hails from the great suburb known as North Oxford, which owes its existence to the great feminine invasion of the last thirty years. This invasion has been threefold: first, there are the families unconnected with the University who have settled here in Oxford as a pleasant centre for concerts, lectures, libraries, museums, and tea-parties; formerly they would have chosen Cheltenham or Leamington. Secondly, there is the married fellow, now a very numerous species, but in the old times a *rara avis*; and lastly there are the colonies of women students. Hence, whereas the town used to come to an end just beyond St. Giles's Church, it now spreads over nearly the whole space between the canal and the Cherwell, and extends northwards for two miles till it includes the once rural hamlet of Summertown.

H.A. Evans

A Shooting Party, Blenheim Palace

27 November 1896 – His Grace, the Duke of Marlborough has a shooting party this week. His Royal Highness, The Prince of Wales with other gentlemen were shooting close to the village on Wednesday. Exactly at one o'clock, Her Royal Highness The Princess of Wales, and the Duchess of Marlborough in No. 1 carriage and Lady Randolph Churchill in No. 2 carriage, and other ladies in No. 3 carriage, drove through the village to join the shooting party at luncheon. The school children were drawn up in a line at the bottom of the Play ground, and when the ladies came in sight, I started them to sing 'God bless the Prince of Wales'. The Princess of Wales caused the carriages to stop whilst the singing was going on, and during their stoppage she bowed several times. Half-holiday in the Afternoon.

Combe School Log Book

A half holiday

PUNTING, OXFORD

PORTER, BLENHEIM PALACE

SMITHY, KINGHAM

THE SMALLHOLDER

When the last Small Holdings Act came into operation I learnt with some astonishment, which was, however, only momentary, that no applications were made under it for land by any labourer or poor man in this comparatively enterprising and intelligent village. I knew that our labourers were comfortable; I knew also that the nature of our soil is not well suited for profitable cultivation in small holdings, like that of the vales of Evesham and Worcester not far away. When I came to think over the matter, I ceased to be surprised that intelligent men with regular wages should hesitate to embark on an attempt to support themselves and their families by working a small holding, from which they could hardly expect to put money in their pockets, as they now do every Saturday. Money has come to be essential to them, to maintain their households at the level demanded by respectable village society; and unless they could feel sure of a money profit from the new enterprise they naturally felt shy of undertaking it. . . . Within the last few days (October 1912) I have found another reason suggested. I do not myself belong to that privileged class that is just now entitled to give secret evidence about the land, but my friend, the leading Liberal here, kindly allowed me to see the printed questions sent him, and the answers he was returning. Here I noticed that he accounted for the failure of our labourers to take advantage of the Act by stating their belief *that it would work them too hard*. My Liberal friend is likely to know, for he is himself an employer of agricultural labour. If it be the truth, or part of the truth, do not let us on that account accuse them of laziness. They do steady work for many hours a day, but when it is done they still have some hours before them, and in these they like to read, smoke, and play games. They see how the small farmer works with his family, for we have him here as well as the big one. They know that his life is a continual grind and chronic anxiety, and that he and his sons have a worn and wearied look on them. Their own life is often a gay one compared with his — especially so is that of the craftsman, mason, blacksmith, and carpenter. Education has, in fact, taught our working folk here as in the towns, that life is worth living as well as wearing out. They have learnt to read and write, and incidentally to take interest in passing events, and they do not wish to rise in the morning full of care, and to drop into bed at night wearied out with the incessant work of the day. Such a day, so they believe, and rightly so far as I know, is that of the smallholder who cannot afford to employ the labour of others; and even on Sunday, it is to be noted, he is often at work while the waged man is at ease.

It is not only, however, education that has brought about this result; other tendencies of the time have operated in the

HARVESTERS, SYDENHAM

same direction. The rise of wages, the cheapness of provisions, the almost complete abandonment of the drinking habit by our younger men, and the possession of ready money which is the result again of all these, have minimized discontent, and discourage any hankering after a change of life. I speak of course of Kingham only, for it does not do to generalize from a slender experience; villages differ greatly, not only in different districts, but even in the same neighbourhood. Here, for example, there is no lack of employment of various kinds, apart from that of agricultural labour proper; our two big landlords supply it in plenty, the one at his Homes, the other on his estate, and an engineer in the village, the railway a mile away, and the 'quality' who are attracted hither by good air, good hunting, and a convenient train-system, take both boys and girls into their service gladly.

W.W. Fowler

DRAWING LOTS

''Tis a curious custom, and I don't suppose there's another such custom anywhere in England', said the farmer, and I cordially agreed with him. We were standing knee deep in uncut hay in a large meadow some 70 acres in extent; the hour was 8 a.m. on the morning of Monday last. Readers of the interesting volume in the Oxfordshire Historical Society's series, entitled 'Three Oxfordshire Parishes', viz., Kidlington, Yarnton, and Begbroke, compiled by Mrs Bryan Stapleton, may recall the account of the 'Lot Meadows', and the curious custom attaching to their allotment. The account had quickened my imagination, and when the date came round I determined to be present at the drawing. The morning was grey, and rain threatened, but the air was pure and fresh, full of sweet country scents, as we, a little band of zealous enquirers, cycled out along the dusty road to Yarnton. Wild roses trailed in the hedgerows, the privet was in full flower, and here and there the smell of new-mown hay blotted out the more subtle scent of the flowers. To cycle the whole way was impossible; the public road in Yarnton comes to an end, and merges into a rough grass track, leading to the large meadow where the ceremony was to take place. Along this we walked our machines. At that early hour of the morning the lane was in possession of the farm cows – they herded together in mild surprise, and trotted before far out of their way rather than allow us to pass by. Under the railway we followed the uneven rutty lane to the meadow. Beautiful rushes grow hereabouts, and yellow flags must have made the place gay with colour earlier in the season. Hitherto we had seen no sign of anything unusual; nothing but the animals and the wide-spreading fields met our searching glances, but now the lane abruptly ended at the entrance to the large meadow of uncut hay. We saw three or four empty carts in the centre of the field, and the horses taking the utmost advantage of the growing hay under their noses. In the far distance a little group of men suggested the 'drawing' we had come so far to see.

COUNTING THE BALLS, YARNTON

OXEY MEADOW

This meadow, known as Yarnton meadow is about 70 acres in extent. It stretches to the railway bank at one end; the long line of willows on the further side shows where the Isis flows along its boundary. There is only one entrance to the meadow – the way we had come, and naturally the most popular lots lie where the least labour in carting must take place. Letting our machines lie flat amongst the hay, we followed the track made by the carts till we had passed them, and were well on our way to the little group of men.

The allotment of the meadows is on this wise. On the Monday following St Peter's Day (June 29th), the grass in the meadows is sold by auction, at the Grapes Inn. The handbill of the sale would puzzle an outsider. The descriptions run as under:-

    One-quarter of William of Bladon,
    Three-quarters of William of Bladon.
    One-quarter of Watery Molley.
    Half of Rothe.
    Half of Rothe; etc., etc.

The grass is sold, and on the following Monday the buyers assemble in the meadow and draw lots for the portions they have bought. Thus, the man who has bought 'One-quarter of Watery Molley' has no idea where that quarter will lie till he draws from out of a bag a little wooden ball, on which is written 'Watery Molley'. This haphazard appropriation was in progress as we entered the field. The buyers of the hay had met together, the 'meadsman' had brought the canvas bag holding the balls, and the drawing had begun. Starting from the extreme end of the field, they walk to where a little upright stone marks a 'lot'. Then the bag is opened and someone draws out a ball. Supposing the name on it to be Harry, the man who has bought the mowing grass called Harry has to take the lot on which the ball 'Harry' is drawn, for his. There being only 13 balls, they have to be drawn three, four, or five times in each field, according to the number of 'lots' it contains. It will be seen that it is a perfectly chance lottery, and much good-humoured fun passes as good lots or indifferent ones are drawn. Just as we came up with the group they had reached another of the boundary-stones, and stood round for the 'draw'. The 'meadsman' very kindly offered us the bag, seeing that we were interested strangers. One of us was to draw the ball, and by our venture some one would be bound to take that lot. The responsibility was frightful – but with an inward petition that one might draw the especial ball for the man who wanted that lot, I plunged my hand in, and pulled out a little ball whereon was inscribed in black letters the name 'Rothe'. Immediately, a man said 'That's mine'. A mower with a scythe stepped forward, and with a few sweeps of his instrument cut the hay for about six

One-quarter of Watery Molley

DRAWING A LOT BALL, YARNTON

ADAMS FARM, CLANFIELD

feet in each direction. Then another man came up with a sharp knife, and skilfully cut a large letter on the exposed surface of the grass. The letter was the initial letter of the man who had bought the grass on the lot called 'Rothe'.

THE BALLS

Right across the field we went with the drawers, encouraged by their kindliness, not seeming the least annoyed by strangers coming in and drawing for them. One after the other we drew a ball, as we reached the different stones which marked a fresh lot, and the buyers took our choice without a murmur. We felt it to be intensely kind of them. At last all the balls had been drawn, and the place where we had entered the meadow was reached. Then I petitioned for a personal inspection of the balls, and was allowed to hold the bag and pull them out to look at. In the volume to which I have referred at the beginning of this column the balls are described as coloured balls: the colour has vanished in the course of years, for they are now little wooden balls, beautifully turned, dark brown in hue (this may be the colour described, but looked to me more like the natural hue of the wood), with the name written on each in black letters. No ball has ever been lost; they live in the bag from one year to another, till this curious drawing takes place, when they emerge from seclusion for a few hours to decide the momentous question of allotment. The original reason for the choice of names seems to have been lost. Conjecture would lead one to suppose the names to be either those of the original buyers or of the men who chose this singular method of disposing of the meadow. The names are Gilbert, White, Harry, Bout, Rothe, William of Bladon, Parry, Walter Geoffrey, Bolton, Dunn, Green, Freeman, and most curious of all, Watery Molley – given by Mrs Stapleton as Walter Molly. The corruption is easy to understand, but it has become the general title for that piece of land, for the handbill advertising the sale gives it as: 'One quarter of Watery Molley (in Oxey Meadow).'

In the meadow we were in, the balls had to be drawn three times; they were now replaced in the bag and the drawing began again, followed each time by the little ceremony of the cutting of a small space of grass, and the carving of a large initial letter. Very clean these letters were. I looked at them as we retraced our steps across the field, and they stood out brown and clean cut in the bright grass. The drawing all finished, one last custom remains before the hay is cut. 'Do you not find it very difficult', I had asked the farmer, 'to keep the line of your lot straight?' 'Very difficult,' was the answer, 'if you don't take care you get cutting some of your neighbour's lot.' To help this difficulty to a solution a number of men do what is called 'running the treads'. They tread down the hay in straight lines from the stones to the hedge, or to the river bank, according to the direction in which the lot runs. That

EIGHTS WEEK, OXFORD

done, the proportioning of Oxey Meadow was over, and the hay is usually cut the same day. On Thursday another meadow was to be drawn in the same way, and on Monday the last meadow will be drawn for, in similar manner, at the same hour of the morning. The last meadow is the largest, and the balls have to be drawn five times before the whole field is allotted. In Mrs Stapleton's volume will be found accounts of the riots and disorder which took place in the following out of this quaint custom at the beginning of this century. They arose from the custom of cutting all the meadows on the same day, a plan which naturally brought in an immense amount of outside labour. The change in the times for drawing and mowing took place in 1817. It is now a peaceful and happy pastoral scene, intensely interesting to anyone who cares to consider old customs. It is to be hoped that, queer as the custom is, it will be preserved, for it must have gone on in unbroken succession year after year for more than a century.

Newspaper cutting, 15 July 1899

A BOAT RACE

The Start. 'Hark!' the first gun. Several of the boats pushed off at once into the stream, and the crowds of men on the bank began to be agitated by the shadow of the coming excitement. The St. Ambrose Crew fingered their oars, put a last dash of grease on and settled their feet against the stretchers.

'Shall we push her off?' asked bow. 'No! I can give you another minute' said Miller, 'only be smart when I give the word.' The captain turned on his seat, his face was quiet but full of confidence. 'Now boys, don't quicken,' he said, 'four short strokes and then steady.' The jackets were thrown on shore and gathered up by the boatman, the crew poised their oars, No. 2. pushing out her head and the captain the stern, Miller took the starting rope in his hand, the rope paid out steadily and the boat settled to her place.

There goes the second gun! one short minute more and we are off. You wouldn't say 'short minute' if you were in the boat with your heart in your mouth, and trembling all over. Those sixty seconds before the starting gun in your first race,

STARTING GUNS, IFFLEY

they are a little life-time. It is an awful moment. The coxswain, though almost dragged backwards off his seat, is equal to the occasion. He holds his watch in his right hand with the tiller rope. 'Eight seconds more, look out for the flash,' an intense few moments of waiting and then comes at last the flash of the starting gun. Long before the sound of the report can roll up the river, the whole pent-up life and energy is let loose, and breaks away with a bound and dash which he who has felt it will remember for his life. The starting ropes drop from the coxswain's hands, the oars gleam on the feather and the boats leap forward. The crowds on the bank scatter and rush along, each keeping as near as may be to its own boat. Men on the towing-path, some slightly in advance as if they could help to drag their boat forward some behind where they can see the rowing better, but all at full speed, in wild excitement and shouting at the top of their voices as on they rush jostling, stumbling, struggling, and panting along. For a quarter of a mile along the bank the glorious maddening hurly-burly extends, and rolls up the side of the stream.

Tom Brown at Oxford

The Fine Old English Labourer

Come lads and listen to my song, a song of honest toil,
'Tis of the English labourer, the tiller of the soil;
I'll tell you how he used to fare, and all the ills he bore,
Till he stood up in his manhood, resolved to bear no more.
    This fine old English labourer, one of the present time.

He used to take whatever wage the farmer chose to pay,
And work as hard as any horse for eighteenpence a day;
Of if he grumbled at the nine and dared to ask for ten,
The angry farmer cursed and swore, and sacked him there and
    then.
    This fine old English labourer, &c.

He used to tramp off to his work while town folk were a-bed,
With nothing in his belly but a crust or two of bread;
He dined upon potatoes, and he never dreamt of meat,
Except a lump of bacon fact sometimes by way of treat.
    This fine old English labourer, &c.

Now he laughs their threats to scorn

MOLLINGTON

He used to find it hard enough to give his children food,
But sent them to the village school as often as he could;
But though he knew that school was good, they must have bread and clothes,
So had to send them to the fields to scare away the crows.
    This fine old English labourer, &c.

He used to walk along the fields and see his landlord's game
Devour his master's growing crops, and think it was a shame;
But if the keeper found on him a rabbit or a wire,
He got it hot when brought before the parson and the squire.
    This fine old English labourer, &c.

But now he's wide awake enough and doing all he can,
At last, for honest labour's rights, he's fighting like a man;
Since squires and landlords will not help, to help himself he'll try,
And if he doesn't get fair wage he'll know the reason why.
    This fine old English labourer, &c.

He knows the land would be no use if labour was not there,
And in the profit he insists he'll have a proper share;
And if they will not own the right of him who sows and delves,
He'll tell the farmer and the squire to till the land themselves.
    This fine old English labourer, &c.

They used to treat him as they liked in the evil days of old,
They thought there was no power on earth to beat the power of Gold
They used to threaten what they'd do whenever work was slack,
But now he laughs their threats to scorn with the Union at his back.
    This fine old English labourer, one of the present time.

MR OAKLEY

55

WATERCRESS GATHERING, EWELME

A remarkable and interesting reminiscence of the [Agricultural Labourers'] Union's early activities is worth recording. Arch in his life tells the story. 'There was a small local strike at Ascott in Oxfordshire, and the Carter of a farm there joined the strike without giving the usual notice. The farmer summoned him and got the costs, and then called in outside labour, two men who came from a neighbouring village. The Ascott women who had husbands out of work thought they would drive the men away, and when they came, out marched the women and mobbed them. They dared the men to enter Hambidge's field but although some of the women carried sticks, no blows except tongue-blows were struck. The farmer took up the matter, and seventeen of the women were summoned before the magistrates at Chipping Norton. The sitting magistrates were two Clergymen. In their evidence, the two men stated that so far from being set upon with sticks, they had been invited by the women to come back to the village and have a drink. There might have been a little Hustling, but the labourers after saying 'No, thank you', to the offer of a drink, went to work under the protection of a Policeman. Of course the women pleaded 'Not Guilty', but the magistrates after retiring, came back into court finding them 'Guilty', and passed sentence on Sixteen of them: seven were to be imprisoned for ten days with hard labour, and the other nine were to have seven days' hard labour. This was clearly an excessive and unjust sentence. The Union was prepared for the infliction of a fine, and some one was in court prepared to pay it, but imprisonment with hard labour none were prepared for. When the decision became known, Chipping Norton was turned upside down. The people were raging, for no one had the least idea that such a law existed. The Press took the matter up, and the action of the Bench was unanimously condemned, but the law did not allow the option of a fine.

The Authorities thought it better on account of the riot to have the women driven to Oxford the same evening in a brake, and they were locked up in Gaol about six in the morning. The feeling was intense, Petitions for their release were sent up to the Home Office and an appeal was made to the county and the public generally. Subscriptions to the amount of £60 came, £5 of the sum in pence, 'and we arranged,' says Arch, 'that the sixteen women should have Five pounds each. When their sentences had expired, we got two four-horse brakes and went to meet them as they came out of Oxford Gaol, and took them right into Ascott headed by a band of music. When we arrived in front of the farmer's house we pulled up and gave each of the women Five pounds.'

H.W. Taunt

LAY'S QUARRY, HANBOROUGH

THE STONEMASON

He was not a native of those parts, but had been brought there a few years earlier by a firm of builders engaged in the restoration of some of the churches of the countryside. He was an expert workman and loved his craft. It was said that he would copy some crumbling detail of carving and fit it in in such a way that the original carver could not have detected the substitution. . . . By the time the restoration work was finished he had married and had two children and, though he never cared for the hamlet or became one with the little community there, as his wife and children did, he stayed behind when his workmates left and settled down to work as an ordinary stonemason.

There was still a good deal of building in stone going on in that part of the country. One country house had been burnt down and had to be rebuilt; another had a new wing added, and afterwards, he would make a tombstone, build a cottage or wall, set a grate, or lay a few bricks as required. Workmen were expected to turn their hands to anything within the limits of their trade and he who could do most was considered the better workman.

Flora Thompson

JAMES WELLER

AN OXFORD INTERIOR

Oxford Fashions

I married Mr Thomas Humphry Ward, Fellow and Tutor of Brasenose College, on April 6, 1872, the knot being tied by my father's friend, my grandfather's pupil and biographer, Dean Stanley. For nine years, till the spring of 1881, we lived in Oxford, in a little house, north of the Parks, in what was then the newest quarter of the University town. They were years, for both of us, of great happiness and incessant activity. Our children, two daughters and a son, were born in 1874, 1876 and 1879. We had many friends, all pursuing the same kind of life as ourselves, and interested in the same kind of things. Nobody under the rank of a Head of a College, except a very few privileged Professors, possessed as much as a thousand 'a year. The average income of the new race of married tutors was not much more than half that sum. Yet we all gave dinner-parties and furnished our houses with Morris papers, old chests and cabinets, and blue pots. The dinner-parties were simple and short. At our own early efforts of the kind, there certainly was not enough to eat. But we all improved with time; and on the whole I think we were very fair housekeepers and competent mothers. Most of us were very anxious to be up-to-date, and in the fashion, whether in aesthetics, in house-keeping, or education. But our fashion was not that of Belgravia or Mayfair, which indeed we scorned! It was the fashion of the movement which sprang from Morris and Burne-Jones. Liberty stuffs very plain in line, but elaborately 'smocked', were greatly in vogue, and evening dresses, 'cut square,' or with 'Watteau pleats,' were generally worn, and often in conscious protest aginst the London 'low dress,' which Oxford – young married Oxford – thought both ugly and 'fast.' And when we had donned our Liberty gowns we went out to dinner, the husband walking, the wife in a bath chair, drawn by an ancient member of an ancient and close fraternity – the 'chairmen' of old Oxford.

Mrs Humphry Ward

HUNT MEETING, BAMPTON

TALLY-HO

The gentry flitted across the scene like kingfishers crossing a flock of hedgerow sparrows. They saw them sweeping through the hamlet in their carriages, the ladies billowing in silks and satins, with tiny chenille-fringed parasols held at an angle to protect their complexions. Or riding to hounds in winter, the men in immaculate pink, the women sitting their side-saddles with hour-glass figures encased in skin-tight black habits. 'Looks for all the world as if she'd been melted and poured into it, now don't she?' On raw, misty mornings they would trot their horses through on their way to the Meet, calling to each other in high-pitched voices it was fun to imitate. Later in the day they would often be seen galloping full-stretch over the fields and then the men at work there would drop their tools and climb on the five-barred gates for a better view, or stop their teams and straighten their backs at the plough-tail to cup their hands to their mouths and shout: 'Tally-ho: A-gallop, a-lye, a-lye, Tally-ho'.

Flora Thompson

THE REVD CHARLES DODGSON

Another silk hat which I well remember . . . always a sleek and respectable one, was that of 'Lewis Carroll' – to give him his proper name, the Revd Charles Dodgson, student of Christ Church. I was just of the generation to appreciate as a boy *Alice in Wonderland* and *Through the Looking Glass*, which I read at school with glee, and ere I came to Oxford I knew most of Dodgson's verse by heart. What a surprise then to find this purveyor of joys for young and old, when he was identified, to be an austere cleric, always dressed in the correct garb of a clergymen of low-church tendencies – sober black, with a waistcoat cut rather low, a large, well-arranged white tie, and an impeccable tall hat. He looked severe to the passer-by, and no one outside the limited sphere in Christ Church in which he moved would have suspected him of being the author of such cascades of riotous fun as the ballad of the 'Walrus and the Carpenter', or the White Knight's dolorous ditty about the 'aged, aged man a sitting on a gate'. I had always supposed Edward Lear to be supreme in the composition of nonsense poetry, but had to own frankly that even the fate of the

TOM QUAD, CHRIST CHURCH, OXFORD

Jumblies or the Woes of the Yonghi Bonghi Bo moved me less than Dodgson's lyrics. Lear's effusions were gems, undoubtedly, but unset gems. Lewis Carroll's verses were gems set in appropriate filigree work of priceless value. The White Knight's Song gathered additional attraction from the character of the White Knight himself, and all his inconsequences.

I suppose that very few readers of the 'Alice' volumes or the *Hunting of the Snark* realize that Dodgson was not only in holy orders, but a very distinguished mathematician . . . I think I must confess that he was the only mathematician that I ever knew who enjoyed an overbounding sense of humour – enough to humanize fifty mathematicians of the normal sort. But students of his scarce and forgotten *opuscula* know this well: one of the most notable of them is the pamphlet on 'the Evalution of Π', which renders into mathematical terms the whole of the long dispute about Dr Jowett's salary as Professor of Greek, in cryptic but unmistakable jibes. Another of his lost brochures is the one entitled 'The Tunnel and the Meat-Safe' – a bitter criticism of some rebuilding in 'Tom Quad' of which he greatly disapproved.

I wish that I had ever had the chance of studying Dodgson in personal intercourse – but save that I saw him once or twice in the Common-room of Christ Church I cannot say that I was ever in touch with him. I think that I was no more unlucky than others – for he moved in a narrow circle, and only unbent with the children whom he loved. In some ways he must have been a lonely being, for when he died no relations cared to take possession of his belongings, and they were disposed of by auction in Holywell Music Room – including all the quaint costumes of the White Rabbit, the Knave of Hearts, and Humpty Dumpty, cut to children's size, and a large collection of photographs of Christ Church people and buildings. They ought never to have come under the hammer. His memory will always live as the contributor to English literary humour of characters like the Hatter and the March Hare, the Duchess, or the White Queen.

Sir Charles Oman

SOULDERN

Traditional Customs

The only days now kept with special customs in Souldern are 14 Feb., 29 May, the Feast Day, and Christmas. On Valentine's Day the children come round shouting – with outstretched hands, and laying great accent on the last line of the distich–

> Good morrow, Valentine!
> I be yours and you be mine,
> Plaze give us a Valentine.

May Day, although shorn of some of its glories by the intolerance of the Puritans, is still May Day, for groups of children, dressed in their Sunday best, go from door to door with their pretty and often most tastefully arranged garlands, bright with kingcups and daisies and all the bravery of spring flowers, chanting the following quaint old ditty –

> Gentlemen and Ladies,
>   We wish you happy May,
> We come to show our May Garland
>   Because it is May Day.
>   *Chorus* – Because it is May Day, &c.

> A branch of May we bring to you
>   And at your door it stands,
> It is but a sprig, but it prospers a bough,
>   The work of our LORD'S hands.
>   *Chorus* – Gentlemen and ladies, &c.
>   *repeat 1st verse.*

On the 29th of May, the anniversary of the restoration of King Charles II, a large branch of oak is displayed in the principal street, and oak apples are extensively worn. On this day also the annual meeting of the Souldern Club or Friendly Society is held. This Club was originally established in 1816, but has been worked under a new system with great success for the last few years. There are at present (1886) 84 actual members who pay an administration fee of 5s., and 4s. per quarter, and 12 honorary members, who subscribe from 10s. to one guinea per annum. Michael Blencowe and Jesse Lake are the stewards, and James Tingey treasurer and secretary; trustees, Messrs. Hill and Welford. The allowance during illness is nine shillings per week for one year, and half pay for any time of sickness afterwards. At the end of every five years the surplus fund, with the exception of £1 per head, is divided in proportion among the members. Those who have

THE GREEN, SWERFORD

received more than the amount in sick pay, forfeit all claim in the division.

The Village Feast or Wake is kept on the first Sunday after the 18th of September. In all probability it was originally held on the first Sunday after the 8th, that day being the anniversary of the Nativity of the Blessed Virgin, to whom the Church is dedicated. We are told that as late as the middle of the present century Souldern feast was looked forward to from September to September. Open house was kept from Saturday till Monday; rich plum puddings were made and joints of beef cooked by all who could afford them, and the poorest cottage had its cake and bottle of home-made wine. Relations and friends from all parts flocked in, old friendships were renewed, and old differences made up.

The observance of the 5th of November has almost become a thing of the past; a contemptible bonfire just serves the purpose of collecting a few roughs.

Christmas is still kept up in somewhat of the olden style; carol singers and mummers come round to all the houses for more than a week beforehand. What the plot of the modern performances may be we are at a loss to say. There is a female called 'Molly', always represented by the biggest young man who can be found; a fight in which some-one is killed, and the doctor comes in on his hobby-horse to bring the deceased to life. Then 'Molly' has the tooth-ache and the doctor operates on her, and extracts a tooth the size of a decanter stopper. His man 'Jack' is in active attendance, and the Clown or Jack-pudding introduces himself in the following terms –

> Ear comes I, as never come yet,
> With my gret yead, and my little wit;
> My yead is gret, my wit is small,
> I'll do my dooty to plaze you all.

As to costumes, the actors appear to have robbed every scarecrow in the parish; and as to the play, it is difficult to say which is most to be wondered at – its intense stupidity or extreme vulgarity.

Oxfordshire Archaeological Society, 1887

STRIKE, BLISS TWEED MILL

Trade Unionism

The strike now in progress at Chipping Norton is of exceptional significance. Wages in Oxfordshire are notoriously low. The Oxford tram strike of last year showed conclusively that there is no hope of improving the deplorably bad conditions of workers in Oxford unless there is a general upward movement in the surrounding country districts. Till the country worker is better off, he will always be tempted into the towns to take the place of any town worker who endeavours to raise his wages. On the other hand, it is from the town worker that the country labourer must learn the lesson of combination. The Workers' Union has realised this and set itself to organise the rural workers along with the scattered industrial workers in the small country towns. This strike is the first trial of trade-unionism in rural Oxfordshire since the days of Joseph Arch, and upon it depends the whole future of the Oxford workers. The rural labourer on market-days hears at first hand how the strike is faring, and his attitude to trade-unionism will depend on its success. Already, in the town itself, the strike has resulted in the formation of branches of three unions, the Carpenters, the Stonemasons and the Painters. The Workers' Union itself is continually gathering members.

THE FACTS

Chipping Norton is a small market town in North Oxfordshire. Down to November last year a few railwaymen, members of the National Union of Railwaymen, were the only trade-unionists in the place. In that month the Workers' Union formed a branch among the employees of Messrs Bliss's tweed-mill. This is the only factory in the town, and employs about 380 hands all told. A week or so afterwards the manager informed the Chairman of the branch that the firm objected to the workers joining an 'outside organisation', and suggested that he and some others might have to choose between leaving the Union and dismissal. This threat had no effect. The management then called the workers together and suggested 'that if thought desirable an employees association be formed, all employees over twenty-one years of age, both male and female, to become members automatically, and *are not to become members of any other union or outside organisation of similar character. No contribution to be payable.*' This association was to approach the management 'in a proper spirit'. Naturally enough, the workers resented this attack on their right of combination, and the offer was refused. Three prominent members of the union were then dismissed. Several deputations interviewed the management and the union organiser also communicated with the management, but re-instalment was refused. Two hundred and fifty out of the three hundred and eighty employees then came out on strike.

The strike has now lasted nearly three months, and there have been repeated negotiations down to February 27th. On January 2nd an agreement was drawn up between the

SOUP FOR PICKETS

managing director and an official of the Workers' Union. In this agreement the firm explicitly recognized the Union, and the men, in their anxiety to reach a settlement, consented in the interests of peace to admit that the firm had had 'no intention of interfering with their rights to join a Union'. We ourselves do not agree with this lenient view of the firm's action, and, in any case, this is no longer the point at issue. The settlement broke down over the reinstatement clause, which was very loosely worded. It was understood by the strikers to mean that 'all the workers would return to work as soon as things could be got into running order'. (This would have been possible, even in the deranged condition of the business, if they had followed the invariable custom of the trade for times of slackness, and worked on short time, sharing the work out equally.) The employer, however, took the clause as pledging him only to the re-engagement of about half the men, leaving the rest to be taken on as trade improved. So confident were the workers that their view was the right one, that they offered to submit the terms to arbitration by a Board of Trade official, and afterwards even by an official of the Midland Employers' Federation, and to stand by his decision. *Both these offers were refused by the management.*

The strike dragged on. Renewed negotiations failed to bring about any change in the firm's attitude. Finally, on February 16th, a mass meeting of the strikers, with only a single dissentient, rejected the firm's renewed offer which, as the manager states, was practically the same as that of January 2nd. The latest manifesto of the firm declares that the door for negotiation is now closed. It is clear that their intention is to break the Union at all costs.

HELP IS NEEDED

If ever a strike deserved the support of those who wish to see a change in the status of Oxfordshire labour and of agricultural labour in general, this strike deserves it. Not merely for their own interests but for a wider cause, these men and women workers have faced enormous odds and considerable hardship. Their Strike Committee is urgently in need of money. To all who can do them no other service we appeal for contributions. They may be sent to Mr John Hieatt, The Leys, Chipping Norton, Oxon, or to G.N. Clark, Fellow of All Souls' College, or G.D.H. Cole, Fellow of Magdalen College.

Pamphlet, 1914

SCHOOL TREAT, UNIVERSITY PARKS, OXFORD

Childhood Walks

Of course we went for walks. Sometimes in the Parks, then a grass field with a cart track across it from East to West, approached from St. Giles' by a footpath between hedges, where Keble Road now is. The Parks were bounded on the North by a path (existing but now closed) which runs along the South side of part of the gardens in the present Norham Gardens; on the South by a cart road and a footpath under Wadham Wall; on the East by a gravel path beside a hawthorn hedge, the remains of which can still be traced by the occasional May trees across the Parks from North to South, near the Cricket Pavilion; on the West by the existing raised path under the old elm trees in Parks Road. A rutty grass road ran below between Banbury Road and Broad Street, the portion of it between South Parks Road and Trinity Gate was a private road, protected by posts from wheeled traffic. Towards the Cherwell, behind the hawthorn hedge, lay agricultural land – Mesopotamia only came into existence about the time that the Parks were extended.

Two terrors lay in wait for me in the Parks, Mrs Routh and the Rag and Bone man. Mrs Routh, widow of the all but centenarian President of Magdalen, was in my eyes a terrifying, bearded old woman, the living example of the witches I read of in fairy tales, whose influence on the young was always harmful. It is true that she rode in a bath-chair and not on a broomstick, but I felt no confidence that the difference of conveyance meant security for me.

The Rag and Bone man's beat lay along Love Lane under Wadham Wall towards his home in Park Passage, whither I was assured, as I fully believed, he would carry me off in his sack if I misbehaved. I often pass Mrs Routh's gravestone in Holywell Cemetery now, and it still surprises me to read on it that she was not seventy when she died.

Then there was Port Meadow. The Black Bridge across the railway frightened horses but gave thrills of agreeable terror to the young who dared to stand upon it as the trains passed below. Between the Black Bridge and Medley a walk had lately been raised above floor level – we knew it as 'Dicky Greswell's walk.' The Rev. Richard Greswell had had this work undertaken during hard times, I believe at his own expense.

Later, when our legs were longer, the new iron bridge

WALTON STREET, OXFORD

across the main stream of the Thames at Medley, opened the way to Binsey and Godstow. I think that it was about this time that the upper Thames was made navigable, the lock at Godstow built, or repaired and the Ford at Binsey deepened to enable Mr. Campbell's beetroot to be transported by water from Lechlade. The Banbury Road was a favourite walk; it offered opportunities for mild adventure and had no terrors. Beside it on the East, between St. Giles' School and the Crescent, lay disused gravel pits; then came Park Town and a large Nursery Garden. The footpath after that rose and bore somewhat to the East; posts protected it from all but foot passengers and perambulators. It led to the East between cornfields and a copse which had grown up in disused gravel pits beside the high road where there were certain yew trees, easily climbed and very popular. Mr. Dayman, a Solicitor, lived at Cherwell Croft, 128 Banbury Road, an eccentric, very clever man, who worked late at his office in St. Giles'. He was terrified to walk alone in the dark at night through this copse, and had an arrangement with the local policeman to meet and see him home through it. Beyond all this lay Summertown, then a remote village.

To the north of St. Giles' Church there were the few old houses on both sides of the Banbury Road. What is now called The Old Parsonage was occupied as cottages.

On the West came one of the larger stone houses, 'standing in its own grounds' (now part of the Acland Nursing Home); after that gardens and allotments as far as the North Parade.

The North Parade, Park Town and the Crescent were in various private ownerships and were built many years before St. John's College and Mr. Bull developed their north Oxford estates. Two nice houses in their own grounds lay between the North Parade and Rackham's Lane (now St. Margaret's Road) The Lawn and The Mound. Of these The Mound is now absorbed by St. Hugh's College.

While I am writing about the North of Oxford I will try to describe the changes from Walton Street northwards, greater perhaps than any.

The back gate of Walton House opened on to Walton Street. The Clarenden Press, St. Paul's School, St. Paul's Church and the long wall of the Radcliffe Observatory remained unaltered until the Maternity Department of the Radcliffe Infirmary was opened in 1931. Jericho House (Higgins' Brewery) was the only building of any size amongst a few old houses before reaching the gate of the Jericho Cemetery. Soon after that the road forked Northwards, a right of way track led across allotments known as Cabbage Hill to Dolly's Hut, Aristotle's Well and Port Meadow, or to Rackham's Lane – now St. Margaret's Road. I have been given to believe that this track, now Kingston Road was the route chosen by Charles I when he escaped from Oxford.

To the West ran the way to Port Meadow with the long high stone wall of Lucy's Foundry on the left and on the right a Pound for stray cattle stood near the top of the incline. Just below it was Walton Well (No. 14 Walton Well Road now

GIANT HAYSTACK, COWLEY

stands on the site) a small square stone enclosure of a constant spring which fed a little running brook, a tributary of the canal. I remember seeing the little brook apparently steaming during an intense frost, when all other water was covered with thick ice. My father rented a field which lay behind the Pound and sloped down to the canal. To reach Port Meadow by this route one had to cross a drawbridge over the canal, a dangerous plaything in the hands of mischievous children who often came to serious grief themselves and added to the difficulties of riders by their manoeuvres. The Walton Well bridges have taken the place of the drawbridge, the flat wooden bridge without sides, and the level crossings of the GWR and L&NW Railways. Here the incessant shunting of goods trains delayed the passage of impatient horses on to the lower end of Port Meadow, which was then more or less of a morass for months at a time. The deposit of Oxford refuse upon this ground over a period of 40 odd years has made it suitable for allotments.

F.M. Gamlen

'LEASING'

After the harvest had been carried from the fields, the women and children swarmed over the stubble picking up the ears of wheat the horse-rake had missed. Gleaning, or 'leazing', as it was called locally.

Up and down and over and over the stubble they hurried, backs bent, eyes on the ground, one hand out-stretched to pick up the ears, the other resting ons the small of the back with the 'handful'. When this had been completed, it was bound with a wisp of straw and erected with others in a double rank, like the harvesters erected their sheaves in shocks, beside the leazer's water-can and dinner-basket. It was hard work, from as soon as possible after daybreak until nightfall, with only two short breaks for refreshment; but the single ears mounted, and a woman with four or five strong, well-disciplined children would carry a good load home on her head every night.

Flora Thompson

ALLEN STEAM ROLLER

PENNY FARTHING, GARSINGTON

PENNY FARTHING

Apart from the occasional carriages and the carrier's cart twice a week, there was little traffic on that road beyond the baker's van and the farm carts and wagons. Sometimes a woman from a neighbouring village or hamlet would pass through on foot, shopping basket on arm, on her way to the market town. It was thought nothing of then to walk six or seven miles to purchase a reel of cotton or a packet of tea, or sixpen'orth of pieces from the butcher to make a meat pudding for Sunday. Excepting the carrier's cart, which only came on certain days, there was no other way of travelling. It was thought quite dashing to ride with Old Jimmy, but frightfully extravagant, for the fare was sixpence. Most people preferred to go on foot and keep the sixpence to spend when they got there.

But, although it was not yet realized, the revolution in transport had begun. The first high 'penny farthing' bicycles were already on the roads, darting and swerving like swallows heralding the summer of the buses and cars and motor cycles which were soon to transform country life. But how fast those new bicycles travelled and how dangerous they looked! Pedestrians backed almost into the hedges when they met one of them, for was there not almost every week in the Sunday newspaper the story of some one being knocked down and killed by a bicycle, and letters from readers saying cyclists ought not to be allowed to use the roads, which, as everybody

68

ST MARTIN'S CHURCH, CARFAX, OXFORD

knew, were provided for people to walk on or to drive on behind horses. 'Bicyclists out to have roads to themselves, like railway trains' was the general opinion.

Yet it was thrilling to see a man hurtling through space on one high wheel, with another tiny wheel wobbling helplessly behind. You wondered how they managed to keep their balance. No wonder they wore an anxious air. 'Bicyclist's face', the expression was called, and the newspapers foretold a hunchbacked and tortured-faced future generation as a result of the pastime.

Flora Thompson

ROAD WIDENING

Those who have visited Carfax in Oxford since the year 1897 must have been struck with the great changes that have taken place there in recent times. It is perhaps not so very strange, especially in London, to have an ancient church demolished and carted away; but in Oxford, we are thankful to be able to say, it is a very rare occurrence. Excuses are made to fit an accomplished fact by those who are half ashamed of the deed, such as that it was only a late Perpendicular church which had been altered, and even re-built, in comparatively late times, and therefore it was no loss. It is true, they say, it was the city church from a very early period; but the east end trespassed on the street and was in the way of the traffic . . . it was pulled down to widen Carfax, and the tower alone remains.

P.H. Ditchfield

BURFORD

> O fair is Moreton in the Marsh,
> And Stow on the wide wold,
> Yet fairer far is Burford town
> With its stone roofs grey and old

Sylvanus Urban, Cornhill Magazine

LAKE, BLENHEIM PARK

MARSTON FERRY

IFFLEY ROAD, OXFORD

THE BANK MANAGER

We had a bank at Bicester kept by my friend and school-fellow Henry Tubb (the best and kindest of men that ever lived) which was at heart a charitable institution. As it was the very last of the private banks to survive the process of amalgamation I like now, when most of us are in the clutches of banking firms who treat us on the strict principles of business, to think of the merciful way in which that good man, as the sole owner of the bank, viewed the deficiencies in our accounts. He recognised no such thing as 'charges on account' or 'interest on overdraft', with which so many of us are faced nowadays on examining our Passbooks. In my own case the only way in which he retaliated upon an overdrawn account was to send me a bigger turkey at Christmas or a heavier joint of lamb at Easter! I mention this in passing not only as a memento of a good and kind man – the greatest benefactor that Bicester is ever likely to know – but also with the faint hope that it may catch the eye of some director or manager of the 'Big Five' and induce him to go and do likewise!

Revd G.P. Crawfurd

HEALTHY HOMES

The aspect of the home should be bright and cheerful, and the main aspect should be south-east; it must have plenty of air and light . . . without free circulation of air the house must become stuffy. Back-to-back houses, so common in most towns, are a positive evil; free ventilation is impossible to such places – the death rate of young infants in such places is often great. The larder often does not receive the attention it requires; it should face north, and be most thoroughly lighted and ventilated, and all windows fitted with fine copper gauze. It is a great advantage to have two windows in each bedroom on separate sides of the room. Floors are best laid with simple parquet – on old floors linoleum (also polished) is effective with a few good rugs. Light about a house is as important as air – a great destroyer of disease and other germs. When housewives are over careful of their carpets and curtains, and exclude the sunlight they are shutting out an influence of the very greatest benefit. I should say, up with the blinds and let the sunlight in and flood your rooms.

Builder's advertisement

FOREST HILL

TIMES ARE BAD

South Newington with its neighbours, Wigginton and Swerford, higher up the stream, may be taken as the type of the poorer Oxfordshire village, a type which presents a marked contrast to the well-to-do and populous Adderbury or Bloxham. Swerford, it is true, has its park and great house . . . but Wigginton and Newington consist chiefly of rows of humble cottages, which have suffered little change for generations. As you wander down the village street you are made to feel that times are bad, that the flower of the rising generation has taken this to heart and has departed to seek its fortune elsewhere.

H.A. Evans

COLLEGE WORK

'College Work' for scouts, cooks, bedmakers, etc., naturally falls off very largely in vacation. Colleges vary in the amount of work that they require from their servants out of term. A large proportion of scouts and college cooks get hotel work in the long vacation, which may involve very hard work, but also secures a change of scene. One cook-boy who apparently worked for about fourteen hours a day in his summer hotel, but walked nightly by the seaside for an hour, explained that he felt the expedition to be the treat of the year. Some of the college scouts or their wives keep lodging-houses, which give them occupation out of term, varied by cricket and rowing matches, or decorous games of bowls on the college cricket-ground. Some again are expected to be available during the vacation to attend to any members of the college who may be in residence. The system of payment also varies. Some colleges pay a quarterly salary to their scouts, irrespective of their employment. Others pay them more or less according to the work required from them in term, under the supposition that they will get other work out of term. Where hardship exists it is in the case of lads, unskilled porters, and charwomen paid by the week in term, who may get good wages while employed, but find it very hard to obtain outside work at least in the short vacations. Hence the preference felt by sensible parents for service for their sons under those colleges which find their staff regular work, even at lower wages, throughout the year. College work, however, is in any case so much sought after in the town that little complaint would be made at much harder conditions than exist at present.

C.V. Butler

So much sought after

COLLEGE SERVANTS, OXFORD

COLLEGE SERVANTS, OXFORD

HILTON'S BOOTERIES, BICESTER

Mr C's Budget

Family: Mr C., a carter; his wife; and three children, aged 8, 6, and one year.
Income: Mr C.'s wages, 18s.; lodger, 5s. 6d. net; care of child, 3s. 9d. Total, £1 7s. 3d.
Summary of a Week's Expenditure, July 1909

	s.	d.
Rent	7	6
Food	11	7
Coals, light, washing	2	5½
Clubs, etc	1	8
Debt paid off weekly	2	6
Total	£1 5	8½
Left over for clothes, etc	1	6½

Day	Breakfast	Dinner	Tea	Supper
Sunday	Eggs, Bread, butter, coffee	Roast Mutton, potatoes, stewed fruit	Bread, butter, tea	Meat, bread
Monday	Bread, butter, coffee	Cold meat, potatoes, bread	Bread, butter, tea	Bread, cheese
Tuesday	Bread, butter, coffee	Hashed mutton, onions, potatoes	Bread, butter, coffee	Bread, cheese
Wednesday	Bread, butter, coffee	Cottage pie, cabbage, potatoes	Bread, butter, tea	Cottage pie, bread
Thursday	Bread, butter, coffee	Beef steak pudding, potatoes	Bread, butter, tea	Bread, cheese
Friday	Bread, butter, eggs, tea	Fish, bread	Bread, butter, tea	Fish, bread, butter
Saturday	Bread, butter, coffee	Liver, bacon, potatoes, rice pudding	Bread, jam, tea	Bread, cheese

CO-OP, BANBURY

Mr D's Budget

A Week's Expenditure, when in Work (1909)

Saturday	s.	d.
Sugar, 4 lb.	0	8
Butter, ½ lb.	0	7
Cheese, ½ lb.	0	4
Lard, ½ lb.	0	4
Bacon, ½ lb	0	6
Tea, ¼ lb.	0	4½
Eggs	0	4
Candles and matches.	0	2
2 loaves	0	6
Flour	0	3
Husband's sick-club	0	7
Meat, 3½ lb.	2	3
Vegetables	0	5
Milk for week	0	7
Monday		
Rent (5 rooms)	5	6
Coal	1	1
Insurance for family	0	10
Dispensary for wife and children	0	2
Loaf	0	3

Tuesday	s.	d.
Soap	0	3
Soda	0	1
Starch and blue	0	1½
Rice, 1 lb.	0	2
Loaf	0	3
Wednesday		
Meat, 2 lb.	1	0
Potatoes	0	2½
Cabbage	0	1
Loaf	0	3
Thursday		
Quaker oats, 1 lb.	0	3
Jam, 1 lb.	0	4
Loaf	0	3
Currants, ½ lb.	0	2
Cocoa, ¼ lb.	0	4½
Friday		
Fish, 1½ lb.	0	6
Light for week (1d.-in-slot gas)	0	7
Salt, pepper, mustard	0	1½
Blacking	0	0½
Wood	0	2
Loaf	0	3
Total	£1 1	2

Summary

	s.	d.
Light, coals, washing materials	2	6
Food	11	7
Rent, excluding poor-rate	5	6
Insurance and clubs	1	7
All else	3	10
Total	£1 5	0

Family: Mr D., a painter's labourer, at 6d. an hour, 'earning an average wage between March and November of 25s. a week' (November to February, broken work); Mrs D., children, 5½, 3½, 6 months looking healthy and well cared for.

The unalloted 3s. 10d. would be spent on boots, clothes, and other things – e.g., the poor-rate of about 7s. a half-year, and parish saving-cards, upon which Mrs D. had paid 13s 9d., and Mr D. £1 2s. 6d., by weekly instalments between February and November.

C.V. Butler

KEEPER, DAY'S LOCK

MAY DAY, GREAT MILTON

Negotiating a Lock

While the water ran out, the lock-keeper came and gave us that curious literary production, a Thames Lock Ticket. It admits you 'through, by, or over the lock or weir' for threepence. That is, I suppose, you can go through the lock in Christian fashion, drown under the weir, push and pull over the roller if there is one, or drag your boat round by the shore; but whether you come out dead or alive, for any of these privileges the Thames Conservancy will have its threepence.

J. & E. Robins Pennell

Bucknell

The Village Feast is observed on the first Sunday after old Michaelmas Day, October 11th. There is a tradition that it was originally held on S. Peter's Day. The date was probably altered in consequence of the Canon of 1536. On May Day a King and Queen are chosen from among the children. These march with the other children in holiday attire from the School to the Church, where a short service is held. A large garland with doll is carried in the procession. The children carry a collecting box, the contents of which go towards furnishing a tea.

May Day Song at Bucknell

A bunch of May I bring you,
    Before your door it stands,
It is but a sprout, but 'tis well spread about,
    By the work of a mighty hand.
Arise, arise, pretty maidens all, and take your garland in,
Or else next morning when you rise, you'll say I brought you none.

Arise, arise, pretty maidens all,
    And call on God for grace,
Repent, repent your former sins,
    While you have time and space.
A man's but a man, his life but a span, he flourishes like a flower.
He's here to-day and gone to-morrow, cut down all in one hour.

And when death strikes it strikes so deep,
    It strikes us to the ground,
There's not a surgeon in all the land,
    Can cure the deadly wound.
So now I've sung my little May song, no longer can I stay.
God bless you all, both great and small, and bring you a merry month of May.

MORRIS DANCING, HEADINGTON

On St. Valentine's Day the children used to go round and collect money, singing –

> To-morrow, to-morrow, Valentine,
> Mr. March has laid his line,
> Please to give us a Valentine.

The observance of Whitsun Ales was kept up till recent years. The scene of the festivities was the Rectory Barn, and in later years the Parish Pound, where a tent was made with rick-cloths. There was dancing on the ground in front of the barn, as many as fifty couples dancing at a time. There were also morris-dancers, six in number, dressed in white trousers and white shirts pleated before and behind. They were bedecked with ribbons, and had small bells on their legs. They were accompanied by a musician who carried a pipe and small drum (the tabor). The last of the musicians, Joseph Powell, now resides at Hawkell in this parish, as do several of the morris-dancers, the oldest being Henry Coles, now 82 years of age. The morris-dancers were attended by a 'Squire', dressed in motley, and carrying a wand with a calf's tail at one end and a bladder at the other. The Squire had to keep a clear space for the dancers, and also acted as jester, improvising doggerel lines suitable to the occasion, and in honour of the more prominent persons who patronised the dancers. The Bucknell morris-dancers, besides performing in their own parish, made the round of the neighbourhood, going as far as Middleton Cheney.

Oxfordshire Archaeological Society, 1903

THE OLD HOUSE

The old house in Broad Street was in its way unique. It consisted of three houses which had been at some former time joined together. Two of these faced the street, and had lath-and-plaster fronts; the third, at the back, was of much older date, and its walls were over three feet thick.

It was Dr Acland's amusement and delight to improve this curious old place until he turned it into a veritable museum, though it always remained what Mrs Acland used to call it, a rabbit-warren. Entering from Broad Street you came into a narrow hall with a Devonshire settle made of walnut and with panelling as a dado on the walls. This panelling continued down the long passage which led to the dining-room and

John Ruskin and John Acland

JOHN RUSKIN AND HENRY ACLAND

MAGDALEN BRIDGE, OXFORD

libraries, and the doors of the dining-room were also of walnut, and made in the same shops. Out of this narrow hall opened a small room, used as a waiting-room for patients, or for those many people who came on all sorts of errands to the house. The walls of this room were completely covered, chiefly with engravings from portraits, and showed the catholicity of his interests and friendships. Chevalier de Bunsen, John Ruskin, Mr Gladstone, Lord Dufferin, Lord Salisbury, Sir Bartle Frere, 'Ben' Harrison, W.H. Smith, Bishop Jacobson, Professor Max Müller, Mr William Froude, Bishop Selwyn of New Zealand and Lichfield, and many others hanging near together; and on one wall were the engravings of Queen Victoria, the Prince Consort, and their children, given to him by Her Majesty.

Out of this little room opened his small consulting-room or study, furnished in the same characteristic manner. Passing down the long passage you came to the first library. As time went on books accumulated everywhere on every sort of subject, down the passage and up the walls, till at last it was all so full that it was a matter of some difficulty to get in or out at all. Beyond this room was another, built originally as an inner sanctum for himself and his wife. When he asked Mrs Acland what O'Shea the Irishman should carve on the stone mantelpiece of the first library, she at once quoted Wordsworth's lines to the Skylark:

Type of the wise who soar but never roam,
True to the kindred points of Heaven and Home.

And as time went on and they grew older, a final shelf came up from the old home and was fixed in the north library with these words carved on it, 'Rest and be thankful.' In every corner not covered with books hung pictures, photographs and curios. The stairs to the drawing-room were narrow and steep, but could not be improved owing to the presence of a massive chimney-stack; by Dr Acland's ingenuity, however, they were made less dark by means of reflectors. At the top of them stood a cast of Alexander Munro's beautiful figure of Undine stepping on to a water-lily. The drawing-room was a low room with a huge beam running down it. Bookcases stood between each window, and there was a long low one across the end, the newest books on every sort of subject being on the octagonal table near the centre. The walls were so covered with pictures that the paper was barely visible. Here hung Millais's famous picture of Mr John Ruskin, given to Dr Acland after the death of the latter's mother, also two sketches of Rossetti's, 'The Gathering of the Herbs' and 'The Eating of the Passover', a small Turner, the Acropolis at Athens, and many other pictures, by George Richmond and his son, and by less distinguished artists, including many by Dr Acland himself of varied scenes in many countries. This room was the

SCHOOL ORCHESTRA, WATLINGTON

centre of the family life; when Dr Acland was at home he was rarely, unless actually occupied in seeing patients or on business, far away from Mrs Acland's side.

I have left to the last the dining-room and the garden, into which the former looked; it was in the oldest part of the house, with very thick walls and quaint appearance. On either side of a stone ogival arch cut through the wall was painted in the pre-Raffaelite days, in red letters, the old college 'grace', for before and after meat – *Benedictus Benedicat: Benedicto Benedicatur*. Dr Acland had at the end of the room arranged a top light for sculpture, and here hung two casts, one of the Holy Family by Michael Angelo, the other of the Nikê Apteros; and in the centre was a bust of Dante.

The garden ran back as far as Trinity Garden-wall, and Dr Acland's originality and ingenuity were constantly exercised in making it as unlike a square bit of town garden as possible. At the four corners of the little fountain stood four pillars, removed from the Tower of the Five Orders at the Bodleian at the time of its restoration. The garden was constantly used in a fine summer as a second drawing-room, with a man-of-war's awning overhead to keep off sun and shower, and on fine hot nights, Dr Acland delighted in having his simple dinner, or his coffee, out there, and he would sit and chat until long after dark.

J.B. Atlay

THE THREE RS

Specimen Schemes of Work for Classes in Two Local Elementary Schools

(I) A Term's Work for a Class of Girls, Average Age 11–12. (Teacher's Private Scheme)

Reading. – I. Class reading-books. II. *Alice in Wonderland*.
Recitation. – Shelley's 'Ode to a Skylark'.
Writing. – Lessons in penmanship: large and small handwriting.
Composition. – Answering questions in history and geography. Letters: social, business, accounts. Autobiographies. Essays.
Grammar. – Analysis and parsing of simple sentences. Punctuation. Phrases.
Arithmetic. – Addition, subtraction, multiplication, and division of decimals. Practical mensuration involving simple areas. Problems introducing unequal division. Simple and compound practice.
Drawing. – Principles of simple perspective applied to simple straight-edged objects.
Needlework. – Garments.
Physical exercises. – According to Board of Education syllabus.

SCHOOL PLAY, KIDMORE END

Geography. – World as a whole: continents. Flora, fauna, peoples of each. Oceans: physical features. Water: river systems. Climate: causes affecting, influence on productions, mode of life, etc.

History. – Earliest times to Edward I inclusive.

Singing. – Voice training. Songs, sight-reading, scales of C F G Major.

In addition to this the girls take a course in cookery which they attend one morning in each week. They have a daily Scripture-class and play organised games once a week.

(2) Work of Standard VII. Boys, aged 13–14

(So much freedom is now left to head-teachers that no quite representative scheme can be given. The following is an example of the method and of some of the subjects taught at present in a local boys' school.)

History. – The boys would have worked in previous years through the history of England in 'broad general outline', starting at seven or eight with stories of great men, and using local examples of architecture, etc. This year they are (a) doing in outline the industrial history of England, from the manorial system to trade unions and the Insurance Act, and (b) having lessons about central and local government – the aim being to train them to think and to work out cause and effect.

Geography. – In this they should have reached a fair general conception of physical geography, illustrated by modelling in sand and plasticine and by visits to Port Meadow and the Parks while they were in the lowest classes. In standards IV and V they would have done some political and commercial geography, chiefly of Great Britain and the British Empire, avoiding the text-book 'lists of products' and 'heights of principal mountains' and drawing maps constantly. In standards VI and VII they might either do more physical and commercial geography of the British possessions with an outline study of, *e.g.*, the United States and the Great Powers of Europe, or they might spend the year in working with their teacher and a good text-book at geography from the 'human' point of view, *e.g.* questions of trade and transport, man's use of the materials round him, the distribution of population and its reasons. This obviously can give plenty of scope for practice in reasoning, and in looking out for the meaning of everyday events.

SOUTH STOKE

Nature-study. – This is carried on throughout the school, and aims at giving an elementary knowledge of natural history and a living interest in it, fostered by school walks and collections. In standards VI and VII the boys might work out some simple chemical and physical experiments, and do a course of elementary human physiology and hygiene, or have lessons varied according to the season – *e.g.*, in winter on such subjects as 'How the soil is broken up – the action of frost, rain, roots; air and water, oxygen, etc.; the barometer and thermometer; rain and snow.'

Other subjects. – Arithmetic (individual work – the ground having been fairly covered by this stage); English (a good deal of private reading encouraged); drawing; singing; daily physical exercises; woodwork; religious lessons daily, according to the diocesan syllabus.

C. V. Butler

CROWDED COTTAGES

Some of the cottages had two bedrooms, others only one, in which case it had to be divided by a screen or curtain to accommodate parents and children. Often the big boys of a family slept downstairs, or were put out to sleep in the second bedroom of an elderly couple whose own children were out in the world. Except at holiday times, there were no big girls to provide for, as they were all out in service. Still, it was often a tight fit, for children swarmed, eight, ten, or even more in some families, and although they were seldom all at home together, the eldest often being married before the youngest was born, beds and shakedowns were often so closely packed that the inmates had to climb over one bed to get into another.

Flora Thompson

ELEPHANTS, BICESTER

St Giles's Faier

An Oxfordshire folk-lore ditty:

Us cums from Head'nton Quaary, an' sum frum Shotover Hill,
An' sum on us cums fru' Whaately, an' sum all th' way fru' Brill,
Fru' Milton, an' fru' 'Aasely, frum Stad'am an' Talmage Stoke,
Frum out o' th' Otmoor country, an' t'others they cums frum Noke;
We all on us cums to Auxford, brought in by th' ould gray mare,
'Tis only wunce a year us cums, an' that's to St Giles's Faier.

Us meets sum pals frum Yarnton, sum more frum Norligh too,
From Blechinton an' Chalton, where they 'cuts 'un half-a-two',
An' Chalberie an' 'Ooten, frum Wesson-on-th'-Green,
An' sum frum Coate an' Climbly, the only time they're seen;
We all on us rides to Auxford, behind o' th' ould gray mare,
'Tis only wunce a year us cums, an' that's to St Giles's Faier.

An' ther us sees old Boozer, as cums frum Witney taown,
But you maunt chaff him either, or much-about he'll fraown,
An' Jack what hails fru' Bampton, an' Joe what cums fru' Leaow,*
They all hev brought thur lasses, but how I dosen't kneaw;
Somehow um rides to Auxford, behind o' th' ould gray mare,
'Tis only wunce a year um cums, an' that's to St Giles's Faier.

Us mixes in the dancing, for-bye us likes it well,
An' goes to see th' helephant, by goms, ain't he a swell,
Us to th' 'Harse an' Jockey' goes in to have some yale,
An' then us larks about th' faier until it all gets stale;
Then whoam us all goes frum Auxford, behind o' th' ould gray mare,
'Tis only wunce a year, ye kneaw, us cums to St Giles's Faier.

* *'Well sur, I belave us how thay spells un L-e-w, but us calls un L-e-a-o-w fur short.'*

H.W. Taunt

A Freshman

It is perhaps surprising to have to confess that I had never been to Oxford before the day on which I was matriculated, October 10, 1878; for I had seen many less notable English and foreign towns before that day. Hence, on arriving, I got merely a confused impression of broad streets, spires, and arched gateways, before I discovered the oddly placed entrance to New College, at the end of a crooked lane. I had expected something more majestic – though the view of the broad front quadrangle, seen through the porter's lodge, somewhat reassured me. I had to report myself to the Dean – Hereford Brooke George, a burly figure with a spreading auburn beard, around whom nearly forty other freshmen gradually mustered.

I was entirely ignorant of what was going to happen, since I had not the slightest idea of what University life and University ceremonies were to be like. No relative of mine had ever worn the gown, save one uncle, but as he died when I was two years of age, I had no opportunity of gathering academic traditions from him. Nor had I the slightest notion of what 'matriculation' meant.

Our stately dean conducted his party of thirty odd freshmen – six scholars in the ample gown, some thirty commoners in the more skimpy two-tailed commoner's outfit, down High Street and then across Saint Aldates.

When we reached the rather obscurely situated gateway of Pembroke College we were ushered into the hall, where we found the Vice-Chancellor of the year, Dr Evan Evans, sitting in state at the high table with certain vaguely seen officials about him. The cheerful old gentleman duly admonished us in Latin, when we had been introduced to him by our dean, presented each of us with a bound copy of the University Statutes, and directed us to write our names in Latin in the Great Matriculation Book. I remember that I had my first academic puzzle at this moment: how was I to describe my father's status in proper classical terminology? I got no help from the signature immediately above my own, which happened to be that of the son of a knight – *equitis filius* – nor from the penultimate one, whose writer had described himself as *generosi filius*. I chanced *armigeri filius*, which was right enough, as my father did own a shield, and was much relieved afterwards to find that this was the correct rendering of 'Esquire'.

I suppose that I must have been one of very few freshmen who devoted their first evening in Oxford to a conscientious

COVERED MARKET, OXFORD

HIGH STREET, OXFORD

study of the University Statutes. We dined in a hall that was nearly empty – for the bulk of the College was not to come up till the next day. I marvelled at the majesty of the hall, but not at the style of the meal, which was ordinary enough. As I sat between two complete strangers we had little conversation: I fancy that we eyed each other like strange dogs in the street. Then I went, feeling very lonely, to the domicile that had been given to me, one of the two top-storey rooms in the tower of the New Buildings – a lofty pile of Gilbert Scott's – somewhat suggesting 'Scottish baronial' or else a very large station hotel.

Here I spent a good two hours at the delightful Jacobean Latin of the Statutes. I studied *De Reverentia Juniorum erga seniores*, which instructed me that if I met any one above the degree of Bachelor of Arts, I was to step into the gutter *de platea descendens*, and to salute by raising my cap. I discovered that it was a grave offence to carry an arquebus or bombard in the street, but that I might take a bow about with me, *honestæ recreationis causa*. Also that I must avoid at all costs the society of *histriones et funambuli*, which did not terrify me at all, as I had no wish to associate with actors and still less with rope-dancers. And I imbibed a proper conviction of the ubiquity and omniscience of proctors, who would not only pursue me for carrying an arquebus, or colloquing with a rope-dancer, but would detect my delinquency if I entered an inn or wine-shop or engaged in games of hazard, or committed the foppish offence of going about in high boots.

My conceptions of what Oxford might be like were undoubtedly most coloured by the perusal of that ancient work *Verdant Green*, a romance in which bump-suppers, collisions with the proctors, and absurd misadventures with undesirable people – such as ratcatchers – bulked more largely than hints as to the scholastic curriculum, or intellectual converse with one's seniors. The University Statutes seemed to corroborate the probability of such incidents. I felt, in consequence, extremely shy and suspicious, and convinced that Oxford was a place where one might be led into spending a great deal of money, and might make unprofitable acquaintances. I was particularly pervaded with the idea that extravagance and debts to tradesmen must be the normal condition of undergraduate life, and that this must be avoided at all costs.

I can see now that my want of knowledge led me into an exaggerated Spartanism, for which there was no real need: but I have little doubt that it was for my moral profit in the end: for practice in self-restraint is invaluable. I told my mother that I would live on my £80 scholarship, and the £50 exhibition

HOUSEBOAT, HENLEY REGATTA

which was given by Winchester to the head of the roll to New College. And this I succeeded in doing for four years, not without much ingenuity and contrivance in economizing on food, clothing and everything else. Bread and cheese lunches, and cold meat dinners, or rather suppers, in my own room were cheap. As a matter of fact I managed surprisingly well, and enjoyed myself thoroughly, recognizing all through that, as a poor man, I must go short of many amusements and activities in which most of my contemporaries indulged. Fortunately I was never an athlete, which put me out of the way of many temptations, nor had I the least tendency towards soft living or good cheer – the Winchester diet had cured me of that. I managed somehow to buy a good many books, and even a coin or two now and then, as the result of economy in other things.

Sir Charles Oman

Regatta Week

Henley seemed quiet by comparison with the July day when we came down from London and found the river a mass of boats and brilliant colours, and the banks crowded with people, and Gargantuan lunches spread at 'The Lion' and 'The Angel' and 'The Catherine Wheel'. But that was during Regatta week, when Englishmen masquerade in gay attire and Englishwomen become 'symphonies in frills and lace', and together picnic in houseboats, launches, rowboats, canoes, punts, dinghies, and every kind of boat invented by man. It is true that now and then the course is cleared and a race rowed:

> 'But if you find a luncheon nigh –
> A mayonnaise, a toothsome pie –
> You'll soon forget about the race.'

J. & E. Robins Pennell

FROZEN RIVER CHERWELL, OXFORD

Christmas

As we grew older there were dances at Christmas, at which we arrived in Bath Chairs. Most of these were designed for one grown person, and in them two children could be conveyed at a pinch; there was one double Bath Chair in great request, into which a family of tender age could be crammed. . . . Bath Chairs were popular with ladies who dined out, as these chairs were admitted within College gates and guests could so avoid a possibly wet walk to the place of their entertainment.

Monsieur d'Egville gave us dancing lessons in the Old Masonic Hall in Alfred Street, High Street, so that when Christmas came we could thread our way through the mazes of Quadrilles, Lancers, the Tempete and Sir Roger. Then we danced the Deux Temps, Valse and the Gallop. The Trois Temps and the Polka came in after I was out . . .

I can only remember being invited to one Christmas Tree in my childhood, consequently an unforgettable event. We had 'Snapdragons' then at home. In a dark room a shallow dish full of brandy and raisins was set on fire, and, greatly daring, we snatched the fruit from the flames. Before the brandy was burnt out salt was thrown into the dish, the effect of which was to turn all faces green; a mild enough amusement.

F.M. Gamlen

Snowballs

I moved down from my eyrie in the Tower to a set of rooms in the Front Quadrangle, where I was quite in the centre of College life. These were excellent rooms, but (as I was to find) had one serious drawback. The next winter happened to be a snowy one, and the quadrangle was white for many weeks. Now snowballing is as attractive to undergraduates as to schoolboys, and impromptu fights were always going on. But any wild hurler of the missile who missed his aim at a friend, was liable to send it against the opposite wall, of which my windows formed an appreciable if not a very large part. For

MAY DAY, IFFLEY

several weeks I was vexed by the occasional crash of one of my panes, and the arrival of a more or less disintegrated snowball on the table at which I was writing. It was impossible to get the glass replaced till next day, and I had to close my shutters, let down my blind, and work by lamp-light till next morning. Moreover the matter was expensive – for the College did not pay for broken glass – on some theory, I suppose, that undergraduates were all more or less prone to snowballing, and should settle the bills caused by their pranks out of their own pockets. I should not like to say that I never took part in a snow-fight myself, but I can conscientiously assert that I never broke the windows of anyone else. Of course we on the ground floor were the only sufferers – those who dwelt aloft were immune from the nuisance.

Sir Charles Oman

School Fashions

Most of the children were clean and at least moderately tidy when they left home, although garments might be too large or too small or much patched. 'Patch upon patch is better 'n holes' was one of the hamlet mothers' maxims. The girls wore large white and coloured print pinafores over their ankle-length frocks, and their hair was worn scraped back from the brow and tied on the crown or plaited into a tight pigtail. Laura appeared on the first morning with her hair pushed back with an Alice in Wonderland comb under a pork-pie hat which had belonged to one of her cousins, but this style of headgear caused so much mirth that she begged that evening to be allowed to wear 'a real hat' and to have her hair plaited.

Flora Thompson

RIVER THAMES, OXFORD

ISIS

In those days the business life of the place centred almost entirely in the University. In term time everyone was busy; when vacation came there was scarcely any business at all. In consequence, from the end of June till the beginning of October there was hardly anything doing here. The colleges were almost empty, the rooms all closed; there were no conferences, nor vacation classes, nor anything of the kind, such as now, to bring people here. Except on Wednesday, cattle market day, and Saturday, the general market, Oxford was almost a desert. The grass used to grow up between the pebbles in the High Street.

Naturally those who could get away, and could find work elsewhere, took it. When I began to tramp England with a knapsack on my back I was constantly greeted by Oxford college servants who had gone off as managers or waiters or cooks to hotels in holiday resorts. Those who did not go away to work seldom went for pleasure. The annual distant holiday was hardly thought of. The usual treat was a day out to Nuneham or to Woodstock. In the latter case they went by road, in the former by water, and it was here that the chief use of the house-boats came in. On the 'flash' days, Tuesdays and Fridays, which were the days on which Nuneham was thrown open, we nearly always saw one or more house-boats going down with their party of holiday-makers and a fiddler or so aboard, just as now we see like parties on the steamers, the only difference being that this was the only form of holiday, whereas now it is but supplemental to the more serious effort.

But to explain what flash days were. I don't know whether they still continue; I suspect not, but in old days they were very important. It was whilst the Thames Commissioners had control of the river, and before the Thames Conservancy had taken it over and done so much dredging. The consequence was that there still remained shallow places which the many deeply-laden barges of the time could only get over if the water was almost bank high. To meet this the river was divided into six sections. In No. 1 and No. 4 sections the weirs were shut down on Saturday and Sunday so that the water might accumulate and fill the river. No. 1 was from Lechlade to Oxford, and on the Monday the barges worked on this section both up and down, in each case letting the water down, and so filling the next section. Next day, Tuesday, it was our flash day and the turn for the barges between us and, I think, Goring. The next was down perhaps to Henley, and so on, whilst, meanwhile, Lechlade was getting ready to

SALTER'S YARD, OXFORD

start another flash which reached us on Friday. So these two days, Tuesday and Friday, were the days not only for barge traffic but also for water parties.

There is another thing which I suspect the Conservancy, by their dredging, may have stopped, but I am not certain, as it is so long since we have had a severe winter, and that is the formation of 'ground ice', ice that is that forms on the bottom of the river. When I spoke to my Science Master about it he talked about the maximum density of water, and told me that the thing was impossible, but I took him down to the river and showed him, opposite the barges, the bottom all coated with ice. I think he was annoyed, but at the river for behaving so unaccountably – indecently even, he seemed to think – and not at me. He was so far right that in a lake or in a river of uniform depth the ice cannot so form, but in the Thames in those days there were deep reaches followed by banks of gravel over which the water was shallow. In time of frost the heavier warmer water sank and remained in the deep parts, and what flowed on was the lighter water at or close to the freezing point, and when the crystals formed in this they attached themselves, as forming crystals will, to any solid they could find; in this case to the gravel at the bottom.

This ice rose from time to time in spongy masses, bringing with it some of the gravel, and floated on until it reached the lock. Here it packed, and if the frost continued, formed a thick solid mass of rough ice which, as more came down, extended further and further up stream; and it was on this ice, far more than surface ice, that on three occasions which I remember a coach and four was driven from Folly Bridge to Iffley. Owing to the deepening of the river I doubt if this will ever again be possible, though at Binsey, the other point near Oxford where I have seen ground ice form, it may still do so.

And here, before finally leaving the river, I would say a few words about the floods. These are with us still, but only as a passing phase. They come and are gone again, but when I was a boy they came but did not go, but were with us as a rule almost all the winter. The weirs were in the first instance the creation of the millers. Even before the Norman Conquest men had begun to throw dams across the stream so as to get a head of water to work the mills, and in consequence laws had to be passed to secure the due passage of boats up and down. The weirs came first, the locks, whether, as in early days, mere gaps in the weirs or, as later, pound locks, came afterwards. The main point is that the weirs, until quite recently, were built not to let down the water but to keep it back, and they did this effectually. In consequence every considerable rain brought out the floods; a big rain or melting snow, great

FLOODS NEAR OXFORD

floods, which filled the whole Thames Valley and were only able to pass away very slowly.

One consequence of this was the splendid skating which we then enjoyed whenever there was a sharp frost. It was seldom in the winter season that there were not floods out, and frequently there were great floods, so that we could skate for miles across the fields above and below Oxford, knowing that the ice would not fail us until the frost broke up. Now we but seldom have floods ready for the frost, and even when we have, and are able to get a little skating on the meadows, we know that only a day or two after the rain has ceased the water will begin to fall rapidly and our ice will be reduced to mere cats' ice. Port Meadow, when flooded, provided the best skating of all, for if there was no snow to spoil it it was one grand sheet of smooth, hard ice from Wolvercote to Medley.

Sometimes we had the floods but no frost, and then was the time for sailing on Port Meadow. The sailing boats of the period were mostly centre-boards, which were moored at ordinary times just across the mouth of the Cherwell where the Pembroke and Magdalen and other barges now stand. When a big flood came these were taken up to Medley where the whole meadow

RIVER BANK, SHIPLAKE

HAYMAKING, KELMSCOT

had become a lake, a shallow one, it was true, but that did not matter, as if the boat passed over any rising place in the ground the centre-board was just forced upwards and fell into place again as soon as deeper water was reached.

One result of this prolonged flooding was the ancient fishy smell which pervaded the river-side when the waters subsided, and which was characteristic of Oxford in the Lent Term. This came from the decomposition of such plants as had been killed by their long immersion and of the Oxford sewage which the floods had spread over the fields. This, with the silt brought down by the waters, was the cause of the heavy hay crops for which the meadows were then noted. These crops were hand-mowed with scythes by gangs of men, of whom the Appleton mowers were the best known, who swung together from early morning till late at night, keen to get the grass down as soon as possible and to pass on to another job. We saw, too, real haymaking in those days. The meadows were full of men and women tossing, and raking, and turning, and pitching – the hay ever on the move. Now it is cut down by a machine and left, then perhaps turned once by another machine and left again, and then it is looked upon as 'made'. I wonder what the horses of old days who knew the genuine article would have said to it.

RIVER THAMES, SHIPLAKE

W.E. Sherwood

NUNEHAM COURTENAY

Visitors' Day at Nuneham

I hardly know how long it took us to get to Nuneham. The whole morning we loafed by the bank while great barges, with gaudily painted sterns, were trailed by slow horses against the current, and men for pleasure towed their skiffs, lifting the rope high above our green top; the sailing boats hurried before the wind, and camping parties, with tents piled high in the stern sculled swiftly past. As we drifted on, the flat pastures gave way to woods, and by and by we came to Nuneham, the place of the Harcourts, better known the world over as the picnicing ground for Oxford parties during Commemoration Week. There is a very ugly house which fortunately only shows for a minute, and a beautiful wooded hill which grows on you as you wind with the river towards it, and get nearer and nearer, until you reach the pretty cottages at its foot. It happened to be Thursday, visitors' day, and pink dresses and white flannels filled the woods with colour.

J.& E. Robins Pennell

Commemoration

When I 'came out' in 1874, many of the College Balls were held in the College Halls, though more often in the old Corn Exchange, a large, unattractive chamber on the site of the present Town Hall. There dancing took place on a temporary floor and covered passages were contrived across the yard in front of Nixon's School, between the Corn Exchange and the entrance in St Aldate's, to the old Town Hall where supper was served. Formerly tickets for the College Balls were all by invitation. Afterwards as the standard of entertainment was raised, and the expense increased, relatives would pay the subscription through the member of the college who entertained them. By degrees there was no disguise of the fact that the ball tickets were for sale, though they could only be obtained through a member of the Committee of the College Ball – 'The honour, or pleasure, of one's company was requested' and the price of the invitation was £1 1s.

On the Tuesday afternoon 'everybody who was anybody' went to the Flower Show, held in a college garden. Then the

GARDENER, ST JOHN'S COLLEGE

ST JOHN'S COLLEGE, OXFORD

Flower Show was fashionable and thronged with visitors; now gardening is fashionable and the Flower Show is forsaken. There would be two large tents for exhibits and a first-rate military band played throughout the afternoon. There would be another Ball on that evening. After having danced for two nights from 9 p.m. till 4 or 5 o'clock on the following morning it was rather an effort to get to the Sheldonian Theatre at eleven, where honorary degrees were conferred at 12 o'clock. Then, as now, the semicircle was reserved for Doctors and élite ladies. Other ladies were provided with seats in the middle or ladies' gallery; admitted by tickets and unprotected they were a quite remarkably rude and unscrupulous pushing crowd. The Upper Gallery was then reserved for undergraduates, where they were often witty and amusing, always noisy. Latterly they became so unruly and riotous that a change of some sort was inevitable. The admission of ladies to the Upper Gallery had the desired effect, the exuberant spirits of the undergraduates were restrained but rather at the expense of the spectacle and the wit of the young men.

LADY WITH HER DOGS

WORCESTER COLLEGE OXFORD

BALLIOL COLLEGE, OXFORD

Masters of Arts and their men friends stood in the area. The friends had to be very careful to be well and suitably dressed, or cries and howls from the Gallery would be so loud and incessant that the ceremony would be held up and the offender, wearing perhaps a red tie, would be obliged to withdraw before the business of the day could proceed.

When the Honorary Degrees had been conferred distinguished visitors were entertained at luncheon at All Souls College, where a happy few of the residents would be invited to meet them. After the luncheon came the Free Masons' Fête, held in a College garden, to which were invited the élite of the University and County to meet the honorary DCLs.

Latterly tickets for this fête could be bought through the Committee. The crowd of visitors to Commemoration had outgrown the power of the purse of even the local Free Masons' hospitality; there was room for all in the college gardens, but a first-rate band, glee-singers and good refreshments could only thus be provided for the large numbers of strangers anxious for invitations.

The last Commemoration Ball took place on the Wednesday night. Visitors who were not quite exhausted went

ST ALDATE'S, OXFORD

for picnics to Nuneham on the Thursday; all left on Friday. After that the University of Oxford was practically closed for the Long Vacation which lasted for about four months. College servants took jobs at hotels at the seaside and elsewhere and the shops which supplied the wants of undergraduates put up their shutters. All the shops in the Turl did so. Grass grew between the cobble stones in the streets. An elderly colleague of mine on the Headington Board of Guardians once asked me, 'Do you remember when they used to weed the cobbles in the High Street in front of all Souls during the Long Vacation?' Of course I did.

Another old acquaintance used then to pull up the weeds before the Angel Hotel to pelt his comrades.

In those days there were plenty of dancing men, it was not necessary to make up a party beforehand for the Balls; undergraduates did not go down until after Commemoration. We danced quadrilles, lancers, valses, polkas and gallops to the music of Coote and Tinné and Julian's Bands. The Blue Danube, Strauss's and other valses were most popular and there were no encores. It was not thought proper to dance more than three or four times with one partner. We sat out between dances, but we usually returned to our chaperons (and we all had them then) before each dance began, and our partners were duly introduced to them. We wore tulle dresses with 'waterfall' trains, horribly fragile and liable to tear, but it was bad form to try to hold them up. Reversing in the valse was introduced by some good performers from the USA but it was difficult, considered a vulgar innovation and did not gain favour. I remember a Commemoration when Oscar Wilde was an undergraduate. A lady belonging to his party came to a Ball wearing a sad coloured silk dress, carrying a single lily in her hand; this was the more remarkable then, as bouquets were made of expensive hot-house flowers all mounted on wires, surrounded by a frill of embossed and perforated paper.

The Free Mason's Ball was the prettiest spectacle; knee breeches, silk stockings, coloured aprons and scarves, the white cloaks of the Knight Templar, all contributed to its gaiety. For the round dances a cord was stretched across the long ball-room during the crowded hours. We danced much faster than the young people of to-day. Coat tails flew by at an angle, shirt collars were often changed during the evening, and satin shoes were worn through.

An immensely fat and highly placed Free Mason, clad in the long White Cloak of the Templars was once helping to form the arch of swords under which the principal guests walked in to supper from the Ballroom. Someone was heard to whisper 'Clothed in white samite, mystic, wonderful', as indeed he was.

F.M. Gamlen

TOLL BRIDGE, EYNSHAM

EXPLORATION

I had much time on my hands while I was reading for Moderations, as one could not be studying the prescribed books all day. Starting with a pocket-map I explored the roads and villages for some eight or ten miles around Oxford, seeking for medieval tombs or interesting details of architecture, up to the limits of Abingdon, Dorchester, Bicester, Woodstock, South Leigh and Stanton Harcourt. The roads were very empty in those days before the motor made them lively and dangerous. But the most curious reflection is that I used to get field-walks in what are now districts completely overrun by new Oxford suburbs. In 1878 Canterbury Road was just being built – beyond it there were only farms and market gardens. There was no building along the Iffley Road after the first 200 yards from Magdalen Bridge. In what are now Grandpont and New Hinksey there were not twenty scattered houses, till one came to the curious little row of cottages called Cold Arbour; and along the Seven Bridges road there was not a dwelling till one reached Botley. Striding along without any need to take care of the traffic, I dreamed many dreams, and formed many plans for the future – of which some of the most obvious were never to be realized – e.g. that I might get a fellowship at New College and continue my Wykehamical traditions – while certain other aspirations, far more unlikely, have come to fruition in unexpected fashions.

DORCHESTER

Sir Charles Oman

A bicycling trip

HOPCROFT'S HOLT INN

DEDDINGTON

BURFORD

Nine-tenths of their lives were spent indoors

NORTH STOKE

QUILTS AND CUSHIONS

> While broken tea cups, wisely kept for show,
> Ranged o'er the chimney, glistened in a row.
>
> *Goldsmith*

To the women, home was home in a special sense, for nine-tenths of their lives were spent indoors. There they washed and cooked and cleaned and mended for their teeming families; there they enjoyed their precious half-hour's peace with a cup of tea before the fire in the afternoon, and there they bore their troubles as best they could and cherished their few joys. At times when things did not press too heavily upon them they found pleasure in re-arranging their few poor articles of furniture, in re-papering the walls and making quilts and cushions of scraps of old cloth to adorn their dwelling and add to its comfort, and few were so poor that they had not some treasure to exhibit, some article that had been in the family since 'I dunno when', or had been bought at a sale of furniture at such-and-such a great house, or had been given them when in service.

Flora Thompson

DORCHESTER

PUNTING, OXFORD

A MODERN DON

The days of port and peace are gone,
I am a modern Oxford Don;
No more I haunt the candled gloom,
The cosy chairs of common room;
Each day the peal of marriage bells
Tradition's gathering mist dispels;
Our life's more complex daily grown,
And no man calls his soul his own.
Myself, a man of modest mark,
Make my snug nest beyond the Park;
Pay twice the rent my means afford,
Spread the too hospitable board;
Each new device earns hearty greeting:
I lecture to the summer meeting,
To day for County Council standing,
To morrow Volunteers commanding.
With good spoon meat (Heaven help the fools)
I feed my pupils for the schools;
Choked with the stodgy stuff I cram 'em,
They face their fate and I exam 'em,
Meanwhile the long expected tome,
The book to justify my claim
To Thinker's or Historian's name,
At last emerges from the type.
And when we're out, my wife and I
Swing gaily on – a-down 'the High'.

Anon.

Nuisances from dust-heaps and pigs

THE CROSS, BANBURY

Dr Buchanan's Report on Banbury: 1870

In visiting the smaller streets and courts of the borough, much room for sanitary improvement was seen. Continuing nuisances from dust-heaps and pigs were mentioned in my former Report . . . and such nuisances seem now to be worse than formerly. No improvement has been made in the method of supplying water to closets. In respect of cleanliness of houses and of subletting, the town certainly does not now deserve so good a character as was given to it in 1866. Here are some illustrations of these statements:

In Foundry Square, Neithrop, twelve houses, with large families and some lodgers, have only three closets, each being used by some twenty or more people. Each closet has a pan and trap, but no service-box or cistern. In Catherine Wheel Yard, in the middle of the town, a slaughter-house was found dirty and badly paved. Pigsties and filthy manure heaps were seen. Some of the houses hereabouts have no back openings to them; and, even if there is a back-yard, it is not made use of for getting ventilation to the house. Back-yards were seen dirty, and the stink-traps in them out of repair. In another slaughter-house at the end of Bowling Green Lane were an accumulation of horribly offensive guts. Cherwell Terrace, formerly a footpath over fields, is greatly in want of paving; its houses again have no back openings. There is one privy to four houses, and no water for the privy nor for domestic use except such as is fetched from a pump in an adjoining garden. About the pump, and giving easy opportunity for befouling the well-water, is much filthy ground, with various dirt heaps, a pigsty, and an old privy and cesspit. In Mill Lane there are again no back windows or other openings to the houses. One water-tap, with Company's water, and furnishing supply for drinking as well as other purposes, is situated inside a common privy which is used by the tenants of five houses and by anybody else who pleases. Here the houses are a good deal sublet, with a family on each floor or a lodger in each room. The back-yard is ill-paved and filthy. This row of houses has been condemned by the Local Board as not fit for habitation, and has also been condemned by the Court-leet; but is still allowed to remain, and is one of the most thickly populated places in the town. At the entrance of Globe Court a heap of refuse was found at 1 o'clock p.m., not yet removed by the scavenger. The yard is extremely ill-paved. Hardly any houses have back openings. Water is supplied to this court by public taps situated so far from some of the houses as not to give reasonable facilities for the water being used. One closet here

MARKET PLACE, BANBURY

is a service box, out of order; others require water to be thrown down by a paid. Many houses too have no through ventilation, yet often have two families to the house. Close by is Calthorpe Court, extremely ill-paved and badly kept, with a great refuse-heap and a pigsty in it. Here is Rossi's Common Lodging-house, from which one fatal case of relapsing fever was taken to the workhouse. The store-place of a rag and bone dealer in Calthorpe Street abuts on this Court, and is, with very good reason, complained of. Heaps of bones were seen lying uncovered in the sun, and quantities of rags in bundles and loose heaps gave out a very nasty smell.

Some of the slaughter-houses, to the number of six or eight, are licensed; but the smaller butchers are allowed to kill in unlicensed places. The slaughter-houses above mentioned were both licensed. The substitution of a public abattoir for all private slaughter-houses has been advocated at the Local Board, but the scheme was abandoned on account of the opposition from the butchers.

About two years ago there were outbreaks of enteric fever in Gatteridge Street, and in a suburban row of houses named Regent's Place, under circumstances which gave the strongest suspicion that the shallow wells, which at that time furnished the only water supply for the inhabitants of those places, had received the soakage of privies. Town water has since been introduced into Gatteridge Street, but Regent's Place has still no water except from its pump-well.

In the Banbury Workhouse there were, in the first four months of the present year, twenty-three cases of relapsing fever, three of which had a fatal issue. Of the twenty-three cases, ten were admitted while suffering from the disease; and thirteen, including two nurses, were in persons previously resident in the Workhouse.

Report of 1870

EWELME

Distress

I knew a man when I was a boy who had a nice property at Filkins he went to a Lawer to borrow £5 he was a very drinking man the Lawer told him to bring his deeds as security he took them and had the money he went again after some more and the Lawer told him to bring that back as he owed. he knew he could not and so he still kept the deeds untill the man died and the property was sold by his Lawyer for a very little and the party as purchased it has now had it over 20 years there is now law now for a little man and heaven knows there are lots of little men being robd daily by some or other of these Lawers and now I have been renting this Farm of an Agent one Mr Price of Burford for as much as 27 years and now for many years I have worked hard early and late for nothing at all and what little property I have got goes yearly towards paying them their rent so in 1876 he died and the next year I gave up the Farm after living there nearly 30 years and losing well nigh £406 and worked like a horse and now 1878 I find no end of Farmers in much the same place. now here is 1879 and this is a wetter season than ever for four seasons there has been no land cleared and prices of corn so low that nearly all Farmers are giving up their Farms and now at the time I am writing there is a inquiry by parliament into the existing distress of the Farmers and afore long there will be an inquiry into the distress of the Landlords and here has been a conservitave Government with a Majority of one hundred and have never attempted to do the least thing for the Tenant Farmers but they passed an act to do away with all the turnpikes and put all the expences of the Roads on the ratepayers and one Brewer I have heard saves one thousand pounds a year in turnpikes alone.

Thomas Banting

CRICKET TEAM, WHEATLEY

VILLAGE CRICKET

A few of the youths and younger men played cricket in the summer. One young man was considered a good bowler locally and he would sometimes get up a team to play one of the neighbouring villages. This once led to a curious little conversation on his doorstep. A lady had alighted from her carriage to ask or, rather, command him to get up a team to play 'the young gentlemen', meaning her sons, on holidays from school, and a few of their friends. Naturally, Frank wanted to know the strength of the team he was to be up against. 'You'd want me to bring a good team, I suppose, ma'am?' he asked respectfully.

'Well, yes,' said the lady. 'The young gentlemen would enjoy a good game. But don't bring *too* good a team. They wouldn't want to be beaten.'

Flora Thompson

AN INDEPENDENT VILLAGE

There is undoubtedly something fascinating about Kingham, as every one who has been here will allow. Its fresh air and breezy situation have something no doubt to do with this; but there is also a certain independence and irregularity about it, making it less commonplace than a village of prim cottages well looked after by a large and benevolent land-owner. Such a village is Churchill, on the hill between us and Chipping Norton; and the reader will now appreciate the saying of old John Beacham, who insisted that he would rather be hung in Kingham than die a natural death in Churchill. There are no Beachams left in Kingham now, but I think the sentiment survives. We never have been close allies of the Churchill folks, but have always had more good will to spare for those of Bledington, the Gloucestershire village a mile to the west, squireless and irregular like our own.

W.W. Fowler

Early dawn of the May morning

MAGDALEN BRIDGE, OXFORD

Cowhorns and Choirs

In Oxford, the custom amongst the urchins of the city and neighbourhood, of celebrating the first of May by the blowing of cow-horns, with which they make discordant music, is an old usage, descended to them from time immemorial. A far sweeter one, however, is that which has obtained from a more recent date in the University, namely, the singing of a hymn of praise and thanksgiving to the Trinity from the summit of its highest tower, that of Magdalen College, just as the sun rises above the horizon on this day.

We had tickets, and getting up by moonlight, we started in the early morning dawn for the tower. For two years we had lived opposite to it, and we knew it well. What a beautiful tower it is! with its eight lovely crocketted pinnacles, on which the birds love to poise themselves and sing, a sweeter decoration than any of the sculptor's wonderful imaginings of gnome or griffin or other fabulous creature. This year we had removed to a new residence at some distance from the great tower, and we had a long walk in the clear, balmy, morning air. Some friends and acquaintances were wending their way in the same direction, intending, however, to content themselves with the less lofty 'Founder's Tower', and they advised us to 'avoid the crush' by doing the same. But we were in good time to ascend before the crowd assembled, and after mounting, mounting some two or three hundred very steep winding stairs of wood and stone, we at length came out upon the roof, and there, what a view met our delighted eyes! I have seen many a view from many a tower in various parts of the world; yet none so fair as that of Oxford in the early dawn of the May morning, from the tower of Magdalen College Chapel –

Well! when we had reached the roof of the tower, we found a good many people already there, the choristers in their white surplices, the Fellows of the college, and several of the Undergraduates – amongst them some friends of our own; and cheerful, cheery greetings passed. We went to the embrasure of the parapet and looked into the street – 'the High', the finest street in the world, architecturally speaking, someone has said – and down upon Magdalen Bridge, which had lately been widened, and has lost some of its old-world beauty, but which is still very picturesque. The crowd of townspeople and urchins was already thickening there, and already a few discordant horns broke the stillness of the morning air. Then

MAGDALEN TOWER, OXFORD

we turned to the north-west, and looked towards Oxford, and, oh! what a view it was! The great Tom tower of Christ Church, the big dome of the Sheldonian Theatre, the exquisite spire of St Mary-the-Virgin, and all the magnificent towers and spires, and architectural beauties of this most beautiful city, stood out in clear, sharp, dark relief against the steel-blue sky, in which the moon still shone, like a silver burnished globe. Behind rose the green hill of Shotover, and below, mapped out amongst the grey old abbey-like cloisters and edifices, were the turfed quads, and secluded college gardens; and the beautiful wood-like grove of Magdalen, where the rooks caw in the old elms, and the deer browse as peacefully beneath the trees as though they were far from the busy haunts of men.

Turning again, we could see a little rural hamlet, nestled on a hillside slope; to its right the village of Iffley, with its beautiful old Norman Church. Between it and us fields and meadows intervening, through which meandered the bright silver threads of the Cherwell and Isis.

Softly and sweetly the hymn was sung by the assembled choir (the youngest of them a dear little laddie of eight years old) just as the five pulses of the clock had ceased to beat, and just as the sun had risen clear from a bank of purple cloud above the horizon, the edges of which it had gilded half an hour ago.

From an attic window of a big house we did indeed perceive two maidservants creep forth upon its roof, awakened from their slumbers by the unwonted stir below, and, hiding their dishevelled locks in shawls, hastily caught up, peer curiously about them at the lively scene.

On the tower-top no drowsy forms are found. All is fresh and bright, each countenance eager with admiration, delight, and interest. One or two 'Undergrads', who, in the excitement of the hour, and the desire to keep up 'time-honoured customs', have pitched their college caps and gowns over the parapet, to find them or not, by and bye, in the quad below, look cold and shivery, and oddly gaunt and weird in the pocket handkerchief head-coverings which they are driven to extemporise. The bells ring on, and the tall tower shakes and vibrates beneath our feet so as to cause a sensation of giddiness. But now, the closely packed throng is gradually thinning. It takes long for all to descend the narrow, steep, winding stair.

Leaving behind 'the High' and its dispersing crowd, we

HIGH STREET, OXFORD

gladly turned into the quiet side street known as Long Wall, skirting the remains of what were once the boundary walls of the city – interesting relics, full of attraction, because of their old-world look, and ancient associations. Just beyond is the church of Holy Cross, with its peaceful, picturesque cemetery, and beyond this again, the Park, with its shady walks, and open cricket ground. Here we were met by a poor man, who offered us cowslips, blue-bells, and purple fritilleras, at 'a penny a bunch'.

We passed the poor fellow unheeding at first, but turned back to purchase some of his 'Mayings', thinking his industry deserved rewarding. It was but half-past five, and he must have been out early in the woods and meadows to have got his basket so well filled, and yet he was probably not so early afoot as, in days of yore, were the youth of both sexes, who were wont, we are told, to rise a little after midnight on 'the Calends, or first day of May, and walk to some neighbouring mead, accompanied with musick and the blowing of horns; where they break down branches from the trees, and adorned them with nosegays and crowns of flowers. When this is done, they return with their booty homewards about the rising of the sun, and make their doors and windows to triumph with the flowery spoil. The after-part of the day is chiefly spent in dancing round a Tall Poll, which is called a May-pole, which being placed in a convenient part of the village, stands there as it were consecrated to the goddess of flowers.'

B.B.

NORTHMOOR

CRAYFISH

One well-known native of these Oxfordshire streams at any rate has for generations afforded sport – of a kind – to the villagers. This is the crayfish, hereabouts called *crawfish*, a delicacy which the local connoisseur pronounces superior to lobster, and for the true enjoyment of which, I am advised that considerable industry is required . . . the sport begins at nightfall, and the method is as follows: certain nets with stiff rims of saucer or basket shape, are baited with liver (if a little gamy so much the better) or herring, and let down into the stream where the fish 'run' in the course of the afternoon. When it begins to get dark the fisherman visits the nets armed with a long hooked pole; with this he lifts and examines the nets one by one, and puts the fish into a wallet, taking care to catch hold of it in such a way that it cannot seize his fingers with its nippers. There is considerable uncertainty as to the amount of the bags, – the crayfish, by the way, are always reckoned by the score – sometimes you may have to wait a couple of hours before the fish are 'on the run', and then suddenly you may catch them as fast as you can lift the nets and pick them out; a friend tells me he has taken a score out of a single basket. As soon as the evening's sport is over, the bag is carried home and the contents emptied into boiling water with salt in it; next morning you may begin your feast. For this sport one of the best rivers is the Glyme.

H.A. Evans

MATRIMONIAL RELATIONS

I knew well that the matrimonial relation, once entered into, is almost always faithfully kept, as I believe it is in rural life generally. What I did not know was that there is a positive opinion about it, and that this may find expression in peculiar ways. A husband and wife, recently married, had had differences; the wife believed, and with reason, that her husband was making away with the bit of money left her by her father, and she took advantage of his absence for a few days to desert the place, locking up the house, and sending all his belongings to the station to await his return. This desertion was more than the village, especially the women of it, could put up with. One evening soon after this I was entering the village from the station, and was surprised to find women, children, and youths lining the road, and making a most horrible din with old pots and pans. I was told that the offending wife had reappeared, and had taken refuge in a cottage hard by; to express their disapproval of her, the population had resorted to that curious process which is described under the name of 'Skimmington' in Mr Hardy's *Mayor of Casterbridge*. This is the only record I have of any such proceeding here, but it was plain that the feeling and the traditional mode of expressing it had remained fully alive in the minds of the people, unknown to the 'quality'.

W.W. Fowler

Work and play

BICESTER

SYDENHAM

CORNBURY

WYCHWOOD

Within a five-mile radius of Charlbury, there is said to be a greater variety of wild flowers than in any other such area of the United Kingdom. . . . At this season [July], when the colours are gaudy on the fields, Wychwood is carpeted with gold; three feet high stands the yellow mullein overtopping the ragwort, and close and low along the ground is the rock cistus. Only in the deepest patches of bosky undergrowth is the colour wanting; in the wide spaces where is nothing between the oaks and the sea of bracken, and on the open heath, it spreads. All through the days of July Wychwood is undisturbed, and in its wide spaces you may wander from dawn to dark with only pheasants and rabbits as your fellows. In the broad lights and grass rides you may come on a stray human being, but following the foot-tracks, the courtesy of breast-high bracken must be solicited for entrance. . . . Beautiful at all times of the day, Wychwood is most marvellous at the hour of sunset.

HEYFORD   *M. Sturge Henderson*

Sources and Photographic Details

While I have made every effort to contact all copyright holders, both authors and publishers, in some cases this has proved impossible, and to them I apologize. I would like to thank the following publishers for permission to use material: Basil Blackwell Ltd for W.E. Sherwood, *Oxford Yesterday*, M. Sturge Henderson, *Three Centuries in North Oxfordshire*, and W.W. Fowler, *Kingham Old and New*; Oxford University Press for F. Thompson, *Lark Rise to Candleford*. For permission to quote from the Combe school log book I would like to thank the Governors of Combe School.

TEXT

All of the page numbers given below relate to pages in this book, and not the page numbers of the source books.

Sources of the text are as follows: H.A. Evans, *Highways and Byways in Oxon. etc* pp. 19, 46, 72, 112; *Transactions of the North Oxfordshire Archaeological Society* (1871) p. 24; Flora Thompson, *Larkrise to Candleford* pp. 29, 57, 59, 67, 68, 69, 83, 90, 103, 108; M. Sturge Henderson, *Three Centuries in North Oxon* p. 114; W.W. Fowler, *Kingham Old and New* pp. 40, 48, 108, 112; F.S. Thacker, *The Stripling Thames* pp. 26, 44; J. & E. Robins Pennell, *The Stream of Pleasure* pp. 14, 44, 77, 88, 95; *Victoria History of the County of Oxfordshire*, volume II pp. 30, 43; *The Pelican* p. 24; *Cornhill Magazine* p. 69; P.H. Ditchfield, *Memorials of Old Oxon* p. 69; *Reports of the Oxfordshire Archaeological Society* pp. 38, 39, 61, 77; [Anon.] *A visit to Witney & Witney Mills* p. 32; F.M. Gamlen, *My Memoirs* pp. 65, 89, 95; H.W. Taunt, *Oxford Illustrated by Camera and Pen* pp. 84, 104; *Tom Brown at Oxford* quoted in above p. 53; J.B. Atlay, *Henry Acland – A Memoir* pp. 27, 78; H.E. Counsell, *37 The Broad* p. 39; W.E. Sherwood, *Oxford Yesterday* p. 91; Sir Charles Oman, *Memories of Victorian Oxford* pp. 40, 59, 85, 89, 100; Mrs Humphry Ward, *A Writer's Recollections* pp. 22, 31, 58; T.F. Plowman, *Fifty Years of a Showman's Life* p. 18; Charles G. Harper, *Thames Valley Villages* p. 20; C.V. Butler, *Social Conditions in Oxford* pp. 72, 74, 81; B.B., *Some Oxford Customs* pp. 14, 109; Revd G.P. Crawfurd, *Recollections of Bicester* p. 71; Bodleian Library, G.A. Oxon. c 250/iv (builder's advertisement) p. 71; Bodleian Library, G.A. Oxon. 4° 360, no. 19 (Dr Buchanan's Report) p. 105; Bodleian Library, G.A. Oxon. c 317/6 (pamphlet, 1914) p. 63.

Newspaper sources: Bodleian Library, G.A. Oxon. c 317 (15), **newspaper cutting p. 53**; *Oxford Mail* **p. 49**; *Oxfordshire News* **p. 23**; *Witney Gazette* **pp. 19, 30, 31.**

Manuscript sources: Combe School log book pp. 13, 46 (deposited in Oxfordshire Archives); H.W. Taunt, 'Joseph Arch and the Labourers' Union' p. 54, (courtesy of the Centre for Oxfordshire Studies; Thomas Banting, 'Reminiscences of Filkins' p. 107 (courtesy of the Centre for Oxfordshire Studies).

ILLUSTRATIONS

The following list of illustrations is in page ascending sequence. Unless otherwise stated the photographs used are from the Oxfordshire Photographic Archive, part of the Centre for Oxfordshire Studies, housed in the Central Library, Oxford.

Front cover, Market Place, Witney, 1900. Front endpaper, Fire brigade on parade in Broad Street, Oxford, 1880. Page i, Thame High Street from south-west, 1904. Page ii, Sibford Gower, c. 1900. Page ii, The merry-go-round, St Giles's fair, Oxford, 1895. Page iii, Camping by the River Thames, c. 1900. Page iv, St Giles's fair from the tower of St Mary Magdalen church, Oxford, c. 1900. Page 1, The River Thames at Shiplake, c. 1895. Page 2, The Gondola at Henley Regatta, c. 1890. Page 3, Lew church, c. 1900. Page 4, Visitors at the Rollright Stones, 1891. Page 5, Children with May Day garland, Great Rollright, 1907. Page 6, Plush weaving at Shutford, c. 1910. Page 7, Crowds on the river during Eights week, Oxford, c. 1900. Page 8, St Edmund Hall, cricket team, Oxford, 1911. Page 8, Keble College, Oxford, c. 1890. Page 9, Encaenia procession in High Street, Oxford, c. 1900. Page 10, Accident in Marshalls Lane, near Church Enstone, c. 1900. Page 11, Queen Street, Oxford, 12 May 1897. Page 12, The cover of the Steeple Aston Co-operative Society magazine, February 1909; *Bodleian Library, G.A. Oxon. c 317/4*. Page 13, North Aston school, c. 1900. Page 14, Punting on the River Cherwell, c. 1900. Page 15, Day's menagerie at St Giles's fair, Oxford, 1895. Page 16, The bible stall at St Giles's fair, Oxford, c. 1890. Page 17, Crowds at St Giles's fair, Oxford, 1906. Page 18, Taylor's Electric Coliseum at St Giles's fair, Oxford, 1905. Page 19, A farmyard, Fulbrook, c. 1900. Page 20, Abel Beesley, university waterman on punt laden with rushes, Oxford, 1901. Page 21, Basket maker's shop, Chipping Norton, 1910. Page 22, Arts End, the Bodleian Library, Oxford, c. 1900. Page 23, Chipping Norton station, c. 1912. Page 24, Ducklington, pond and church, c. 1895. Page 25, Chalgrove, 1904. Page 25, Floods in Thame Park, 1905. Page 26, The ferry at Bablock Hythe, c. 1860. Page 27, The

OXFORDSHIRE *of one hundred years ago*

Radcliffe Infirmary, Oxford, *c.* 1885. Page 28, Floods in Lake Street, Oxford, *c.* 1890. Page 29, Radcliffe Infirmary, Victoria ward, *c.* 1905. Page 30, Cowley, family motoring, *c.* 1900. Page 30, Ploughteam at Sarsden Cross, *c.* 1900. Page 31, Burford, hiring fair, *c.* 1895. Page 32, Tennis in the gardens, Worcester College, Oxford, *c.* 1880. Page 33, Willeying the wool, Witney, *c.* 1900. Page 34, Weighing wool, Witney, *c.* 1900. Page 34, Sheep-shearing, *c.* 1896. Page 35, The loom shed, Witney, *c.* 1900. Page 36, Sheep dipping, Radcot Bridge, *c.* 1885. Page 36, Mill workers, Witney, 1898. Page 37, Whipping the edges of blankets, Witney, 1898. Page 37, Despatching wool, Witney, *c.* 1900. Page 38, The mill, Crawley, *c.* 1900. Page 39, School children at Weston-on-the-Green, *c.* 1900. Page 40, Postmen, Steeple Aston, *c.* 1910. Page 41, High Street, Oxford, 1907. Page 42, Blackwell's shop, Broad Street, Oxford, *c.* 1910. Page 43, Astall, *c.* 1900. Page 44, Children paddling, Cowley, 1914. Page 45, Whitchurch bridge, *c.* 1885. Page 45, Mapledurham mill, *c.* 1887. Page 46, Tea in the garden, Somerville College, Oxford, *c.* 1900. Page 47, Women punting, Oxford, 1895. Page 47, A porter with spaniels, Blenheim Palace, *c.* 1900. Page 48, The smithy, Kingham, *c.* 1920. Page 49, Harvesters, Sydenham, *c.* 1900. Page 50, Counting the lot balls, Yarnton, *c.* 1895. Page 51, Drawing a lot ball, Yarnton, *c.* 1895. Page 52, Adams Farm, Clanfield, *c.* 1900. Page 53, Eights' week, Oxford, 1911. Page 54, Water men with starting guns, Iffley, 1908. Page 55, Hauling timber at Mollington, *c.* 1895; *Birmingham Central Library*. Page 55, Mr Oakley. Page 56, Watercress gathering at Ewelme, *c.* 1895. Page 57, Lay's quarry, Hanborough, 1890. Page 57, James Weller, sexton of Church Hanborough. Page 58, An Oxford interior, *c.* 1890. Page 59, Hunt meeting in the square, Bampton, *c.* 1900. Page 60, Tom Quad, Christ Church, Oxford, *c.* 1865. Page 61, Souldern, *c.* 1910. Page 62, The village green, Swerford, *c.* 1910. Page 63, Police guarding the mill during strike at Chipping Norton, 1914. Page 64, Soup for women pickets, Chipping Norton, 1914. Page 65, A school outing in the University Parks, Oxford, *c.* 1895. Page 66, Oxford University Press, Walton Street, Oxford, *c.* 1880. Page 67, A giant haystack at Cowley, *c.* 1900. Page 68, A John Allen steam roller, Cowley, *c.* 1900. Page 68, A penny farthing, Garsington, *c.* 1890. Page 69, St Martin's church, Carfax, Oxford before demolition, *c.* 1895. Page 70, The lake, Blenheim Park, *c.* 1890. Page 70, The ferry at Marston, *c.* 1887. Page 71, Henley House, Iffley Road, Oxford, *c.* 1900. Page 72, Forest Hill, 1907. Page 73, A group of college servants (kitchen staff), Oxford, *c.* 1900. Page 73, A group of college servants (New College), Oxford, *c.* 1900. Page 74, Hilton's Booteries, Bicester, *c.* 1900; Harris Morgan & Son, Bicester. Page 75, The Co-operative stores, Banbury, *c.* 1910. Page 76, The keeper, Day's lock, 1904. Page 77, Maypole, Great Milton, *c.* 1909. Page 78, Morris dancing, Headington, 1899. Page 79, Henry Acland, John Ruskin, and Mrs Severn, Oxford, 1894. Page 80, Magdalen Bridge, Oxford, *c.* 1910. Page 81, School orchestra and dog, Watlington, 1900. Page 82, The school play (Robin Hood, king of Sherwood), Kidmore End, 1914. Page 83, South Stoke, *c.* 1900. Page 84, Elephants in the street, Bicester, *c.* 1900. Page 85, Undergraduates on the Begbrook coach, Oxford, *c.* 1900. Page 86, The covered market, Oxford, 1909. Page 87, High Street, Oxford, *c.* 1900. Page 88, Houseboat party at Henley regatta, *c.* 1890. Page 89, The frozen River Cherwell, *c.* 1887. Page 90, May Day in Iffley, *c.* 1906. Page 91, Coach and horses on the frozen River Thames, Oxford, 1895. Page 92, Launching a lifeboat at Salter's boat-yard, Oxford, 1900. Page 93, Train caught in floods off Abingdon Road, Oxford, *c.* 1875. Page 93, The river bank, Shiplake, *c.* 1900. Page 94, Women haymaking, Kelmscot, 1917. Page 94, Rowing on the River Thames at Shiplake, *c.* 1880. Page 95, Nuneham Courtenay on fête day, *c.* 1882. Page 96, The gardener, St John's College, Oxford, *c.* 1870. Page 97, St John's College, Oxford, *c.* 1890. Page 97, Woman and dogs, Oxford, *c.* 1900. Page 98, Worcester College, Oxford, *c.* 1880. Page 98, Balliol College, Oxford, 1886. Page 99, St Aldates, Oxford, *c.* 1897. Page 100, Swinford toll-bridge, Eynsham, *c.* 1900. Page 100, Bicyclists at the abbey gate, Dorchester, *c.* 1890. Page 101, Bicyclists at Hopcroft's Holt, *c.* 1900. Page 102, Burford High Street, *c.* 1888. Page 103, North Stoke, *c.* 1895. Page 103, Old woman, Dorchester, 1907. Page 104, Mayoral punt, Oxford, 1892. Page 105, Banbury cross, *c.* 1900. Page 106, Banbury Market Place, *c.* 1878. Page 107, The ford, Ewelme, *c.* 1895. Page 108, Wheatley cricket team, 1907. Page 109, May morning crowds on Magdalen Bridge, Oxford, 1908. Page 110, Choristers on Magdalen Tower, Oxford, *c.* 1895. Page 111, High Street, Oxford, 1899. Page 112, Northmoor, *c.* 1886. Page 113, Tennis in front of the church, Bicester, *c.* 1879. Page 113, Lacemaking at Sydenham, *c.* 1900. Page 114, The walk to Iron Well, Cornbury, *c.* 1890. Page 114, Ladies on bicycles at Heyford, *c.* 1900. Back endpaper, Crowds listening to Magdalen choristers, May morning 1895. Back cover, Meadows by the Cherwell, Marston, *c.* 1900.

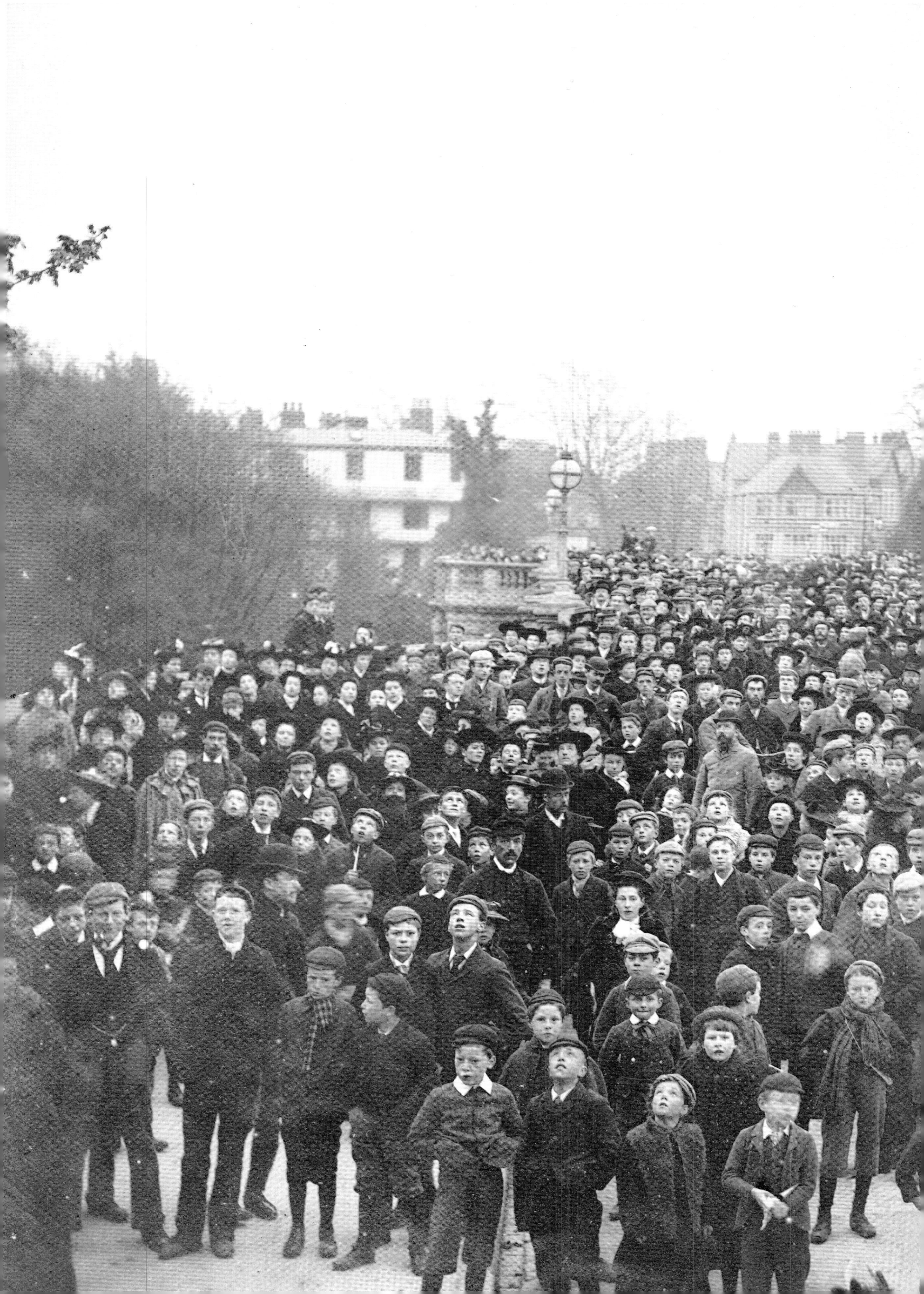